I SPY

ALSO BY TOM MARCUS

Fiction
CAPTURE OR KILL

Non fiction
SOLDIER SPY

I
SPY

My Life in MI5

TOM MARCUS

MACMILLAN

First published 2019 by Macmillan
an imprint of Pan Macmillan
20 New Wharf Road, London N1 9RR
Associated companies throughout the world
www.panmacmillan.com

ISBN 978-1-5098-6409-6 HB
ISBN 978-1-5098-6410-2 TPB

1 3 5 7 9 8 6 4 2

A CIP catalogue record for this book is available from the British Library.

Typeset by Jouve (UK), Milton Keynes
Printed and bound by CPI Group (UK) Ltd, Croydon, CR0 4YY

Visit www.panmacmillan.com to read more about all our books
and to buy them. You will also find features, author interviews and
news of any author events, and you can sign up for e-newsletters
so that you're always first to hear about our new releases.

Dedicated to the families who suffered unimaginable loss.
We stand with you.

Saffie Rose Roussos
John Atkinson
Megan Hurley
Olivia Campbell-Hardy
Alison Howe
Lisa Lees
Angelika Klis
Marcin Klis
Martyn Hett
Kelly Brewster
Jane Tweddle
Nell Jones
Michelle Kiss
Sorrell Leczkowski
Liam Curry
Chloe Rutherford
Elaine McIver
Wendy Fawell
Eilidh MacLeod
Courtney Boyle
Philip Tron
Georgina Callander

CONTENTS

CONTENTS

PROLOGUE

It's the screams you hear first. There are men and women everywhere, from all walks of life, running, hiding, some frozen into petrified stillness. This isn't a normal scene in London, but it's one that is fast becoming anticipated.

Zero Six.

More carnage, as I see glimpses of bodies, the walking wounded and those who have already lost the fight. One or two people are recording what they can on their phones, handsets shaking uncontrollably. There's a flash of the three targets, wearing what look like very crude suicide vests, stalking more prey. The armed police close in, running fearlessly towards the fight.

Zero Six.

Right now, I know that MI5 officers will be reacting to a protocol designed to put every conceivable asset on the ground within minutes. Surveillance teams already on the ground will be re-deployed. Those who had just finished and were at home with their families, or somewhere desperately trying to switch off, will be in their cars and with the teams immediately. The intelligence officers would be briefing the teams live on the radios, no time to bring them in. The operators in the teams, not just surveillance but the technical attack teams, the office geeks within Thames House, our cousins in Vauxhall Cross and the wobbly heads in Cheltenham would be working together with one goal in mind: to stop the killers.

Zero Six, roger, en route.

The first shots ring out, and I know from the controlled manner this is almost certainly the police firearms officers. Over the past few years, due to the huge spike in the scale of terrorist activity and their capability, the Counter Terrorism Unit is now without question the best trained police force in the world. Tonight, just south of London Bridge, they are proving it, as the echoes of gunfire continue to bounce around the buildings, a brutal counterpoint to the screams.

My lungs spasm, gasping for air, as I realize I am frozen with my phone to my ear, waiting for an update from my team leader or the operations officer back at base.

'Breaking news here on Sky, as what's being described as a terrorist attack in the heart of London . . .'

Lowering my phone, I look at the blank black screen. No call. No messages. No longer frozen, I take a step back, soaking in my surroundings. *Fuck.* The TV is on, this is on the news. I'm not on the ground. I'm no longer in MI5. I'm not hearing my radio. It was an auditory hallucination. I've relapsed. *Get out, get out NOW!*

It's late at night and everyone in the house is asleep. I grab the door keys and leave, my legs instantly propelling me into a run I didn't know I needed. Moving faster and faster, I cover the couple of miles to a large wood.

I'm brought up short after vaulting a dry-stone wall that acts as a land boundary to a farm. It's dark around here – the immediate area is almost pitch black thanks to the looming treeline.

As my heart and lungs struggle to replace the oxygen my muscles have burned through, I find myself sitting on this low wall looking towards a break in the trees through which I can see a valley and hills in the distance.

Zero Six.

FUCK OFF, THAT'S NOT ME ANYMORE!

I'm not MI5 anymore but I always will be. I'm no longer part of my team, but I can always hear them. I'm no longer hunting the most dangerous terrorists in the world, but every day I'm watching and waiting for them.

Even moving back along this dark muddy track I'm trying to pick out a route in the shadows that will take me home a completely different way. Some call it paranoia; even the doctors I've dealt with in the past would classify my day-to-day behaviour as paranoid. PTSD or not, the curse engrained into me also keeps me alive.

Spotting a different route to take, I cut across an open field, dark silhouettes of cows moving slowly in the distance. I'm walking rather than running, giving myself time to face the demons I had convinced myself were gone. My mind is calmer by the time I creep back into the house. Resisting the urge to turn the news on, I strip out of my wet clothes and sit on the sofa thinking about the team. They'll be on the ground right now, helping to hunt down anyone associated with the London Bridge targets, anyone who could be waiting for the right time to launch their own attack.

I can imagine the speed at which the intelligence officers on the desk would be shifting through terabytes of live data, creating a triage of threats from thousands of targets.

I can almost hear the radio transmissions, the team leader calling in assets, continuous updates from Thames House, bikers blasting past every operator, all task-focused and doing everything humanly possible to prevent more attacks like this. Unfortunately, you can't stop every single one, it's impossible. And we will get hit again. It might be next week, might be next year, but it will happen. The thing to remember is that our intelligence and military is the best fighting force in the world. Like any world champion, some attacks will find a way through our defences, but we can take the blows and keep fighting. Our guard never drops. Together with my team, I helped stop hundreds of attacks over the years. They continue to do so today.

I wrote about some of my experiences as an MI5 officer in *Soldier Spy*. On the one hand, remembering the past showed me that having PTSD wasn't my fault. I wasn't a victim, just someone who got caught out in the open at all the wrong times. Revisiting my career for *I Spy* has allowed me to describe some of the operations I couldn't include in the first book and go deeper into the challenges that defined me, and the lessons learned along the way.

The memories of my team are so vivid, they stay with me. To this day I want to be back with them and instantly hate myself for it, because going back would take me away from my family. What I can do is remember them in my writing, and pay tribute to the bravery of the men and women of MI5.

1

TRAINING TO KILL

My lungs were burning, the taste of copper in my mouth as my body screamed for more oxygen to feed my muscles or for me to stop. I can't stop. No choice but to keep pushing up the side of this mountain no matter what.

The terrorist training camp was around 600 metres away from me, but I needed a higher vantage point to get clear imagery.

From the quick map study I'd done in the car I knew there would be a good position further up ahead and now, as my soaking wet boots desperately tried to keep enough traction to stop me falling, I could just make out the natural dip in the side of this steep Welsh mountain. From there I'd be able to look directly down on the camp and hopefully have enough cover to enable me to hide.

My eyesight had quickly adjusted to the darkness when I set out but the rocks and bushes around me were becoming clearer now. First light was only minutes away and I had to be in place before all the targets got up for morning prayers.

We'd been investigating them for a year but this was the

first time we'd had this entire cell together in one place. It was a perfect opportunity to get some video footage that would quite probably be used at a later date in court.

Come on, keep pushing! Can't let the team down. I'd been running as hard as I could for a good thirty minutes, leaving the car a couple of miles away and using another valley as cover before starting to run vertically up the mountain.

Fifty metres to go. I stumbled, somehow found my footing again and kept running. Finally at the dip, I dropped down on the dew-covered grass and unzipped my camera bag, which was basically a normal hiker's rucksack that fitted the environment perfectly. I took the long-lens camera out first; this would be my decoy if anyone did see me tucked away here. The actual camera I was interested in was my video camera. I connected the lead to a screen which stayed in my rucksack to prevent it giving away my position in the low light.

My heart was still racing as my body fought to get the lactic acid out of my muscles. Taking a breath and holding it for a second, I slowed myself down, then tucked the video camera on the other side of the bush, angling it roughly in the direction of the three tents below. The targets wouldn't be able to see me at this distance or elevation, but I still had to be careful.

My cover story was really simple and effective. If I did get any interest from ramblers or anyone related to our targets, I was birdspotting after hearing from my mates that this was a good place to photograph hawks and other winged things. Taking a few photographs on my digital SLR, adjusting the settings for low level light conditions, I aimed to dispel any doubt about what I was actually here for. I knew I had to be fairly quiet though; even at this distance sound carries. I was banking on the fact these particular targets weren't that in tune with their surroundings, plus the natural dip I was in and the thick bushes I was hiding behind would dissipate any sound.

We usually found ourselves operating on crime-ridden city streets so being in the Welsh countryside made a nice change of pace, even though a rock was digging into my hip and now I'd stopped sprinting I was cold, my sweat-drenched clothes only making things worse.

Using the touch screen in my rucksack, I zoomed the focus of the digital video camera nice and tight on the tents.

'Team leader from Zero Six . . .' I was still gasping for air and had been motoring up there at full tilt for so long that I was nearly sick. No time for that now though. Snatching a breath, I continued to send my message on my covert radio. 'I have control of the site, can give constant commentary.'

'*Roger that,*' Graeme, our team leader replied. '*Will you be able to ID them quickly?*'

'Yes yes. I'll get them face-on while they do morning prayer.'

I knew they would be facing south-east to pray, the direction of Mecca, and my position was chosen to be near perfect for facial recognition. Watching the video screen, I realized I'd made it just in time.

'From Zero Six, we have movement at the tents, will give targets when I see them properly.' First prayers, like clockwork – these guys were predictable if nothing else.

'Roger that, Zero Six. If you can control them within that little area we'll keep the team out of the valley, ready for a vehicle move.'

Keeping the team away would make the targets feel comfortable.

'Understood, and that's a STAND BY STAND BY, we have GREEN ATLANTIC, WHITE KESTREL out of the most northern tent, both dark trousers, dark tops, carrying prayer mats.'

Staying nice and quiet, I continued to whisper into my radio, burying my mouth into the neck of my wet jacket. Everything we do as operators is with our cover in mind. I couldn't see anyone else around here apart from the tents and two of our targets rolling their prayer mats out, but just because I couldn't see anyone, that didn't mean I couldn't be seen.

As GREEN ATLANTIC and WHITE KESTREL washed their hands and feet prior to prayer, I saw the rest of the cell.

'And stations that's RED HARRIER, PACIFIC LION, BLUE TONGA and COLD SAHARA all out in the open now, all dressed in dark clothing top and bottom, carrying prayer mats.'

'Roger that, Zero Six, thanks.' The team leader was straight on the net to reply, his voice comforting given that I was alone and isolated.

'Team leader from Zero Six, while they are praying I'll keep the commentary to a minimum. Base, this is all recording for your information.'

'Team Leader, understood.'

'*Base, roger.*'

The operations officer back at Thames House was seeing the live feed I was recording so they could analyse it in real time. These officers are highly experienced men and women who feed information to the team leaders, liaise with police and coordinate the teams taking over shifts

The targets hadn't been here long. This training camp was designed to replicate camps normally seen in Syria or Afghanistan in which recruits would be taught weapons handling, how to strip and fire automatic rifles, run over arduous terrain, build home-made bombs and form a bond with each other. The sort of brotherhood seen in the military, except these guys were hell-bent on blowing themselves up if we let them.

All highly educated with degrees, they were out of their comfort zone roughing it miles from anywhere, but it's the type of environment that enhances and cements a certain amount of resilience. The problem we've got is we just can't have resilient suicide bombers.

They finished cleansing themselves and, just as planned, faced directly towards me to pray. Sitting down with my digital camera on my lap, I pretended to rummage around in my rucksack. I needed to zoom slightly tighter in on the targets. This was 100 per cent the whole cell. All in one place, in the middle of nowhere, surrounded and in their eyes protected by the rugged terrain.

It was a strange situation to be in, to see these guys praying together, calmly, almost with a gentleness that suited the early morning of the Welsh mountains. It was intimate and humbling to watch them like this. We'd been on this group for a long time, and were well aware of their desire to kill, but as I watched them on my tiny screen I became a little hypnotized by their softer side.

Time for a quick update to my team.

'Stations from Zero Six, that's the entire group now finishing their prayers and into the tents.'

'Team leader, roger.'

Shit! I was straight back on to the radio,

'All Stations, GREEN ATLANTIC has just given BLUE TONGA a shotgun and a large hunting knife. Ops if you have the live feed can you confirm? I'm not tight enough to be completely sure but it looks like double barrel, wooden stock.'

'Base roger, and we've seen, thanks Zero Six.'

The team leader made sure everyone acknowledged my last transmission. We knew these guys were willing to kill and now we'd confirmed they had the means. The threat to life, immediate to us and imminent to the public, was increased.

Things like this don't scare us; if anything they make us stronger. This might seem arrogant to some, but think about it. When determined, would-be mass-murdering terrorists are coming to kill you, your family, everyone you care about, who do you want standing in their way? Someone who isn't entirely confident in their ability to protect you, or people like us?

We're not superheroes, and we are far from perfect. But right here, right now, there is no one better equipped, both physically and mentally. This whole country is ours, and we protect it day and night.

I was the only operator close to these targets. I was still 600 metres away from them, but in this environment, with the lack of other people around, it was close as I'd dare get. I knew that we'd be calling in the arrest of these guys soon but we couldn't blow the operation now by making them nervous. Letting them think they were completely unstoppable was the perfect play right now. Plus, my team was at best twenty to thirty minutes away from me.

If I was too close to them and they found me, I'd have no chance against six blokes. I'd be dead in minutes.

I was expecting all six targets to prepare breakfast and then either do some sort of training where they were or move onto the hills. With previous training camps we've seen, they nearly always try to fit some sort of hill walk in, probably because they have seen programmes about the special forces doing their selection course in Wales. I wasn't sure what I was seeing but had to prepare the team anyway.

'Stations from Zero Six, just be aware they might be packing up their camp.'

The team leader reacted instantly. *'Roger that Zero Six, keep commentary coming please. Stations close in now, ready for a vehicle move.'*

As I lifted my eyes from the screen hidden inside my bag to take a quick look up at the ridgeline in front of me, the radio transmissions sped up.

'From Charlie Eight Eight, a grey Toyota Previa drove towards

the main [road] about five minutes ago, roughly in the area of the break in the treeline the cell used to walk to their campsite.'

'Any details?' The team leader was keen to find out if the car was connected to this group or not. Thankfully, Charlie Eight Eight was in our team camper van, a gleaming VW complete with side awning and bikes on the back. It had everything you'd need for a weekend getaway in the countryside and was the perfect cover for us. No one in their right mind would think it was an MI5 surveillance vehicle. It was no secret everyone in the team wanted to use it in places like this.

'Negative,' Charlie Eight Eight replied. *'Came in from the east, not sure if the west position spotted it leaving?'*

'West, negative.'

Fuck. These guys were about to be picked up. I knew it. We had everyone in place to control them to their next destination but we didn't know, yet, who the driver of the Toyota people carrier was or where they were going.

The camera made the faintest of whines as I zoomed in to bring the campsite closer to my screen. I needed to let the team know what was happening so they were ready.

'From Zero Six, that's all three tents being packed up now.'

'Base, roger that. Team Leader go to channel nine please.'

The team leader being asked to go to another channel by the operations officer back in Thames House told us there was an update to this operation coming, probably based around this vehicle showing up in the area and our targets packing up.

We'd gathered enough intelligence over the months to take

the cell out: preparations of weapons and explosives, incitement, belonging to a banned terrorist organization, the list was endless.

It was important to let the team and the team leader know what I would and would not be able to do when these guys moved away from the campsite, so I got straight on to the radio again. The chatter between every member of the team was constant now.

'For information, from Zero Six I can control them from here if they do go to the main road to the south.'

'*Charlie Eight Eight, roger that mate.*'

'*Zero Six from Team Leader, what's the latest?*'

'No change, still packing their tents away. Happening fairly quick, won't be long before they have packed up the site.'

'*Great, thanks. Permission for a quick update on Operation UNDERTONE, Zero Six?*'

Every operation has its own specific code name. It's chosen at random and no operation shares the same name, ever. Targets within the operation are given two-word names: GREEN ATLANTIC, BLUE TONGA, for example. We always ask for permission to talk on the net from the person who is in control of the target, as their commentary is an absolute priority.

'Zero Six go ahead.'

'*Thanks. Stations, as you can gather from Base's message to me a minute ago, the desk have made the decision to put in an arrest on this group. We want them in a vehicle to prevent any chance of them running into the hills. Zero Six so far?*'

Sometimes, when we were transmitting a long message, we'd break it with the words 'so far' to check we were still being heard, or to give someone else a chance to cut in if needed.

'So far,' I confirmed.

The image of these guys running around the mountain with armed police chasing them Benny Hill style was making me smile, but it made perfect sense for the strike team to hit them while in the confines of a vehicle, when they would be easier to control. (MI5 operators don't have powers of arrest, which is one of the reasons the police are brought in if targets need to be apprehended.)

'To that end, if Zero Six tracks them towards the main, we'll have Charlie Eight Eight confirm them into the vehicle. Bravo Six will take the vehicle on, guiding the Executive Action team in at the T-junction to put the hard stop in.'

'Bravo' is part of the code name for each of our bikers, while 'Charlie' is used for anyone in a vehicle. 'Zero' means the operative is on foot. My job was now relatively simple: watch, wait and report. I would give constant commentary as the group walked towards the main road out of this valley, hopefully towards a vehicle, so the rest of the team knew what was happening and could take over.

'Charlie Eight Eight, roger.'

'Bravo Six, roger.'

'Zero Six, roger the last. For information all the tents are now packed away. GREEN ATLANTIC looks like he's lost something.'

I could see GREEN ATLANTIC checking his pockets and bags before asking the other targets something, and was thinking to myself it'd be funny if he had lost his house keys, because home was the last place he was going.

Normally we only give a 'stand by' over the radios to wake everyone up to the fact the target has been seen; it stands out from the other type of commentary we give on the net as something important. We don't usually give a stand by when we already have control of the targets but given how important the next half hour was going to be, I didn't want to take any chances.

'STAND BY STAND BY. That's all six targets now leaving the campsite, walking SOUTH SOUTH towards the main. Each has a backpack with a grey roll mat on the top, Zero Six has control.'

Staying in position, nice and still, I zoomed the camera right out using the screen in the bottom of my rucksack. If I started moving now it would show I was reacting to the targets' movement, a clear sign that I was interested in them. Controlling them as much as I could through the video camera would allow me to keep hidden.

'*Charlie Eight Eight roger.*'

'*Base roger and the Executive Action team is in the area now waiting to be guided in.*'

'Roger, they are three zero zero metres away from the main now continuing south.'

GREEN ATLANTIC was still patting his pockets down and glancing back towards the site of their camp. The way they were leaving obviously meant this was pre-planned, especially if the Toyota people carrier that came into the area was for them, and I couldn't help but question why, if he had lost something, he didn't have time to search properly for it.

The six targets were walking quickly through the valley, five of them with their heads down, typical of people who aren't used to waking up early in rough wet terrain. BLUE TONGA's head wasn't watching his feet like the rest; he was looking up at the ridgelines, every so often scanning past my general area.

I stayed still so I didn't give away my position. With the sun rising fast it felt like a searchlight was being cast onto this mountainside, and the only thing hiding me was a large gorse bush and the evaporating dew, which looked like dry ice as it rose off the grass.

The group was now virtually adjacent to me, about 300 metres away. GREEN ATLANTIC had finally stopped fidgeting.

'Stations, targets still towards the main,' I said, lowering my voice even further. 'Base and Team Leader be aware that BLUE TONGA is still the one with the shotgun and knife in his large bag, red in colour. BLUE TONGA is extremely aware of his surroundings.'

'*Charlie Eight Eight roger.*' In the background you could hear Chris cooking some food in the back of the VW, living his cover perfectly. Lucky bastard; I was out here freezing and he was in pure luxury in a nice, dry spanking-new camper!

'*Base roger that. Zero Six, confirm weapon is in BLUE TON-GA's rucksack, and that the colour is red?*'

'Yes yes, red, it's the only red rucksack within the group. All targets dressed in dark clothing, but BLUE TONGA definitely has the red bag with weapons inside. I'll zoom in tighter now so you can see the feed your end.'

I waited a few seconds for Base to analyse the feed as I zoomed in on the back of BLUE TONGA's red bag.

It didn't take the operations officer long to get straight back on to the net. '*Base, have seen, thank you. Passing that on now.*'

Watching the group head towards the natural break in the trees that gave them access to the road, I started to give the team a countdown so they could move into position ready to take control from me.

'From Zero Six, that's now five zero metres away from the main, I'll lose control of them just before they hit the main road.'

Even with the camera zoom, I could only just see the targets.

'Charlie Eight Eight, that's out of sight to Zero Six, all yours.'

'*Charlie Eight Eight, have seen, I have control. That's all six targets towards this grey Toyota Previa – VRN is Mike one six one Tango Golf Kilo. Can't ID the driver. BLUE TONGA and PACIFIC LION have opened the boot and they are loading the backpacks. Base, BLUE TONGA has placed the red bag carefully into the boot of the Toyota, RED BAG INTO THE BOOT. The other targets have placed their bags at the rear of the vehicle and entered.'*

Base would be passing Chris's information about the bag of weapons straight on to the Executive Action strike team. No one was concerned about his proximity to these targets as the underlying noise of a pan sizzling meant he was still well disguised as a camper. I could almost visualize the full English fry-up. My stomach rumbled.

'Bravo Six roger, and ready to take them on when you give them away.'

Paul popped up on the net on his motorbike, ready to take control of the Toyota when it moved. Constantly handing over control between team members means targets never see or suspect they are being followed.

'Charlie Eight Eight, roger. Boot closed and BLUE TONGA and PACIFIC LION are now complete in the vehicle too, that's all six targets into vehicle and lights are on. Team leader, I've got good imagery of this.'

'Roger, thank you. Bravo Six, the arrest team is being guided by Base as soon as you have control.'

I'd have to wait until the police arrest team had secured the vehicle and targets before I could leave this position. While listening to the commentary I continued my cover as a bird watcher, adjusting the camera settings and taking some sample shots of the local scenery. Living your cover story allows operators like us to keep working. We have a saying in our MI5 surveillance teams: a covert operator operates for life.

'*Bravo Six from Charlie Eight Eight, that's target vehicle now driving off away WEST, WEST all yours.*'

'*Bravo Six roger and have seen, I have control. Base for information speed is already four zero, five zero miles per hour.*'

'*Roger, keep control. When they approach the T-junction can you give count down please?*'

'*Bravo Six roger that, speed now six zero, six five miles per hour, one mile from T-junction.*'

Paul would have studied the map as soon as he knew he was responsible for guiding the police arrest team in. The fact the vehicle was speeding out of the area meant it was obviously a good time for us to put the stop in on them.

'*From Bravo Six, vehicle is now half a mile from the T-junction. Base acknowledge?*'

'*Base roger. EXECUTIVE ACTION NOW! EXECUTIVE ACTION NOW! Bravo Six you have a marked SO19 vehicle approaching from the rear, let them through then hold back. They also have teams ahead at the T-junction. For your information this will be a hard stop. HARD STOP.*'

The operations officer back in the ops room in Thames House was cool as ice, but repeating and emphasizing key words like this makes everyone on the ground that much more aware. It's needed when things go loud. A 'hard stop' is a term the police and special forces use when they are arresting a target or targets with armed force and are expecting to face resistance. SO19 is the shorthand used for specialist police firearms units, who are deployed on operations like this as Executive Action teams.

Executive Action teams are fully armed, and over the years the police teams used for these hard arrests have become incredibly skilled. The speed and controlled aggression they use is highly effective, but it's having the discipline to know when to pull the trigger and when not to that makes our police teams the best.

'*Bravo Six roger, and have seen police team, handing over to them now.*' Paul's motorbike engine was just audible under the sound of his calm transmissions. Even though the game was stepping up and shots were potentially about to be fired in front of him, Paul's speech and commentary remained consistent and clear.

Staying still, I was expecting to hear some sort of gunfire or small explosion. With the vehicle moving at speed the team were likely to force it to a stop by using blocking vehicles in front while the armed police of SO19 pulled in behind, blowing the back tyres out.

It didn't take long for the sound of carnage to echo its way across the valley. I counted two clear shots within the rapid echoes and one smaller bang which sounded like a vehicle crash.

'*For information from Bravo Six, the Executive Action team have shot the rear tyres out of the vehicle at the T-junction. All targets and driver being pulled out now.*'

The team leader was instantly on the radio.

'*Team Leader roger that. All stations cease and withdraw. Head back to the briefing room, grab some food on the way, it's a long drive back. Acknowledge down the list.*'

As soon as the police teams have control like this we melt away. We don't want anyone to see us, local passers-by, targets, not even police teams.

As all the vehicle call signs responded to the team leader, I started packing up the cameras. My legs were completely soaked so I was more than happy we'd arrested these guys – I could now get the fuck out of here.

'Zero Six roger, I'll give you a shout when I get back to my vehicle.'

'*Thanks Zero Six.*'

I had a couple of miles to cover to get to my car, but there was no rush now. GREEN ATLANTIC's body language earlier was still bugging me. Was I right that he'd lost something? Whenever you doubt something, there is no doubt – there's just an explanation you can't see yet. Ever since I was a little kid, I've had a need to know what lies behind people's behaviour. I remember walking into my dad's bedroom when I was about six, to tell him there was someone at the door. I caught him quickly stuffing something into the pocket of a jacket hanging in his wardrobe. As soon as he'd left the room I was in the wardrobe snooping. I found a full bottle of vodka (not that I realized what it was) and empty bottles hidden away in his other jackets. People are always hiding something.

Given that the cell had been arrested and I had a bit of time, I could afford to go and walk through their campsite. It would add more distance on my route back but if I carried on along the ridgeline and dropped down onto the area of their site I could check it then carry on walking back towards my car without having to double back on myself.

Slinging the rucksack onto my back, I tightened the straps. The radio was now completely silent apart from one last update from the operations officer back at base.

'*Stations Operation UNDERTONE update, SO19 put in a hard stop on all seven occupants of the Grey Toyota and they are all now in custody. Good job, I'll see you all back at the debrief once you get here. If you're still moving out of the area be mindful of uniformed police cars and a recovery truck moving in to take the Toyota back for forensics. Base out.*'

Job done, all arrested. Hopefully we'd get a fair amount of intelligence from the arrests to bolt onto the massive amount we'd already achieved.

The sun had broken over the horizon and it was officially morning in this part of Wales. I love it here. The harshness of the weather and the terrain, the resilience of the people, makes me think of what life should be like. Simple, co-existing with nature. The reality though is that in this timeless landscape I'd just been watching one of the most current threats to our nation preparing for war.

I'd spotted a natural path about twenty metres lower than the ridgeline that would allow me to drop down into the valley below and walk the route back towards my car via the campsite. It was pretty unlikely I'd find anything there but spending a minute or two searching would put my mind at rest before I had to drive the four to five hours back to Thames House for debrief.

Moving across the mountainside like any other early morning rambler, I kept a close eye on the location of the campsite so I stayed locked into the area. Lighting and perspective can change so quickly in the hills that you could lose your positioning instantly by making a simple mistake like not looking where you're going. Sounds obvious, but it happens all the time. Just keeping your head up fixes these potential problems.

I had to resist the urge to break into a run coming downhill as I made my way down to the valley floor. Terrain like this always reminds me of my military training, especially the Special Operations side of things. Being used to surviving environments where you're already cold and wet and fairly isolated gives you reserves to draw on when you suddenly find yourself switching from inner-city operations surrounded by noise, speed and people to the middle of nowhere playing a game of hide and seek with armed terrorists.

It was easy to spot the campsite. Although there weren't many obvious visual markers, like large trees or a half-broken wall to lock on to, the grass was still trampled from where the tents had been pitched and the scorched earth showed that they had obviously had a fire at some point too.

Putting my rucksack on the grass, I got my water bottle out as if to take a rest. The chances I was being watched by a counter-surveillance team or anyone hostile were extremely remote, but we live our cover until we get back to base. As I took a drink I played back the actions of the targets this morning – where they moved, how they packed up their gear, where they washed their feet and hands before praying. Visualizing it and trying to relive it, I muttered, 'Come on, you fucker, what did you lose?'

Strolling around the site slowly I moved towards the spot where GREEN ATLANTIC's tent had stood. How the fuck did he miss this? Clear as day, right there, sunk into the grass and covered in water droplets. A phone. *Fuck.* I needed to get onto my radio.

'Team Leader and Base, do you read Zero Six?'

'*Go ahead.*'

'Just walked through the site where the targets had their tents on my way back to my car and found a phone in the grass. Could be what GREEN ATLANTIC was looking for.'

'*Roger that, bring it back for the techs to look at.*'

'*Base roger, thanks Zero Six.*'

'*Zero Six, do you read Charlie Eight?*' It was Helen, one of the team.

'Go ahead, mate.'

'*Tom, if that's my camera bag you have, then right at the bottom there is a black waterproof pouch filled with dry rice. I store the memory cards from the cameras in there sometimes if it pisses down. Whack the phone in it.*'

Helen had likely given me the opportunity to save whatever data might be on this phone from being destroyed by the wet conditions. God knows how long it had been out in the elements.

'Legend, thanks Helen!'

Pretending to adjust my laces, I took a knee next to the

phone, grabbed it quickly and stuffed it up the cuff of my jacket, using the velcro strap to hold it in place. It was soaking wet so I was hoping Helen's rice trick worked. Walking back over to my rucksack and placing my water bottle inside, I found the small waterproof black bag of rice. I slid the phone out of my jacket straight into the little bag, which I sealed and shook slightly to ensure the rice surrounded the mobile, giving it the best chance to soak up the moisture. With a bit of luck the techs would be able to pull everything off it. I was just praying it was the thing GREEN ATLANTIC had lost.

Eventually making it back to the car, I started the engine and let the interior warm up before setting off. My trousers were still soaking wet and, given there was no massive rush to get to debrief, I knew I could afford the time. The drive back to London was straightforward and using my cover credit card, issued to all operators, I bought a shitload of junk food, so the journey went quickly as I ate my body weight in burgers, chips and onion rings.

In Thames House, the anonymous grey building on Millbank that is the headquarters of MI5, I took the lift up to the briefing room, sharing it with two women from HR. They knew I was an operator from the way I was dressed, the complete polar opposite to their smart office wear.

Leaving the lift on my floor, I walked straight into the briefing room and was surprised to see only the operations officer and my team leader. It looked like they'd been there a while.

'We've sent everyone home, mate,' Graeme said. He was keen to look after the team and give us time with our families, especially with the amount of hours we'd been doing lately. 'We'll give a full update tomorrow but so far it looks a solid arrest. We've got snippets of intelligence coming through already that they were going to hit a busy cathedral in the city. Have you got that phone you picked up?'

'Yeah, it's still in Helen's bag of dry rice. Hopefully techs can pull something off it. I'm not sure if it is GREEN ATLANTIC's or not, but worth a shot. The cameras are in there too. Video is time stamped in case you need that for evidence.'

'Thanks, Tom. See you tomorrow morning. So far we are back here at half six.'

By the time I got back to my house I'd have roughly eight hours before I had to set off again.

'No dramas, catch you later. I'm on my phone if you need me.'

The video footage I'd recorded of the targets praying outside their tents would likely be used in their prosecution, but all of that wouldn't involve operators like us. Most of the time we are kept away from court cases to allow us to do our jobs on the ground, but right then I didn't give a fuck about the terrorist cell we'd stopped earlier in that remote area of Wales, I just wanted to get home to see my wife.

2

SURVIVAL INSTINCT

I was confident in my ability as an operator for MI5, you have to be. You need to be 100 per cent sure you can do the jobs your team needs you to do, whether it's following a suicide bomber from their makeshift bomb factory all the way to their intended target without being seen, or talking your way out of danger when local drug dealers want to know what you're doing on their turf.

Some confuse this confidence for arrogance. It's not. I never claim MI5, particularly the surveillance officers in A4, are superhuman. We do, however, have a unique set of skills that allow us to keep people safe. We never doubt our reputation of being the best covert surveillance operators in the world and I make no apologies for that. When our country is under attack from thousands of hostile threats, the public need people like us to stand between them and pure, unrelenting evil.

Are we all likeable people? No, of course not.

Are we good at our job? You better believe it!

You can't politely ask our enemies to kindly not blow our

children up while they are at a concert, or offer forgiveness to those who hire a van and mow people down in the street. If the intelligence officers tell us you're a threat to our country and its people, we're going to track you down and every single person helping you.

My early life was the perfect training for my job at MI5. Although a part of me wishes I'd had a normal childhood, if that had been the case I might never have ended up in a job I loved. As a kid, I didn't have any of the security most children take for granted. Instead I learned to recognize and trust the one very basic animal element that is hardwired into our DNA – our survival instinct.

You know when you're in a dangerous situation, the same as any dog or cat does. You can feel something not quite right in the atmosphere around you, either through experience or a simple process of observation. An animal knows when it's time to fight to stay alive or to run away. As a kid you can't always run but I was going to learn that this didn't have to make me totally powerless.

I was sent to a Catholic school, not because my mum and dad chose it but because it was the only local school that had a place. Although a small northern school run by nuns might sound idyllic to some, to others it might suggest somewhere much harsher. The second picture would be right. By a distance. But the school did accelerate the development of skill sets I used as an adult to keep me alive. I remember one cold Monday morning in the middle of January, when I was sitting with the rest of the school on the wooden floor of the assembly hall listening to one of the sisters, who was our school head, talking. I was six years old.

'I hope everyone came to church yesterday,' she said. It wasn't meant to be a question, at least I didn't think so. 'Stand up if you didn't come to church yesterday.'

Well, I didn't go. I never went. I wasn't really sure what church was at that age. Standing up, it took a few seconds for me to realize that everyone, including the three nuns in charge and all the other teachers, was looking directly at me. Completely unaware of doing something wrong, I looked around. I was the only one standing up. Just me.

Was this good or bad? I guessed I was about to be in trouble. I was right. The oldest of the blue-clad sisters pulled me out to the front. One of my black plimsolls fell off as I struggled to stay upright, a combination of being yanked like a dog and having nowhere to place my feet other than on the rows of kids.

'Christ gave his life for all of us. For all of you. We go to church to pray, to show respect and to confess our own sins.' The sister had hold of the back of my neck, her fingernails clawing at my skin. The door out to the schoolyard was closed, the other door leading to the classrooms was blocked by kids and teachers. I was trapped, but my instinct was telling me to run. It was only my young, naive nature that stopped me trying. I'd just lost my front two baby teeth; I wasn't old enough to have the confidence to run. Yet.

'Marcus, you haven't confessed your sins. You have let

yourself and this school down. For that you must be punished
to make sure you stay on the correct path.'

Punished for what? I thought. *How can Jesus love everyone but
punish you if you don't go to church?* Even at this young age I
thought this was odd.

No time to think about it too much. As soon as the vice-
like grip left my neck I felt a sharp fast slap against the back
of my legs. It was so unexpected I jumped forward. Turning
around, trying to understand what had just happened, I saw
the sister holding a wooden ruler. I still remember the sting-
ing sensation.

'Go and sit down, Marcus!'

Making my way over the sea of kids, trying to find the
missing pump for my left foot, I wasn't angry at what had
happened. I wasn't sad either. If anything I was determined
for it not to happen again. By the time I walked myself home
from school, which was a good few miles, I was soaking wet.
Using a key tied to a bit of string around my neck to let myself
in, I knew my dad was home. I could smell him. At that age I
didn't have any idea what being drunk meant nor did I recognize what I was smelling. Today I know it as alcohol, especially cheap vodka, which almost smells like hairspray.

Finding my dad swaying in his chair in the front room,
struggling to see what was on the TV, I innocently asked,
'Daddy, can I go to church? Teachers say to go on Sundays.'

Nothing. As he leaned forwards trying to gain some sort of
balance, I tried again. 'Daddy? Church?'

That was the day I harnessed the ability to spot the

danger signals. Understand the picture in front of you: what's wrong here? What is likely to happen next and how do I survive it?

'CHUURRRRCCCHHHH?!' The slurred word spat out of his mouth, saliva clinging to his lips. He grabbed a fistful of my hair in one hand and my neck with the other, much tighter than the sister at school that morning. I felt myself being lifted off the ground. To this day I'm not sure how I ended up in the back room of the house but I remember flying to the floor from the ceiling and my head leading the way like a plane in a nose dive. Except it was my dad who was accelerating me towards the bare floorboards.

I remember hearing a lot of words I hadn't heard before, a handful of 'fucks' and 'bastard' as I was pinned down before being hit repeatedly over the head with a large book. 'Da . . . Daddy . . .!'

That's the last thing I remember, saying 'Daddy'. This is the first time I've admitted this took place. I didn't even tell the psychiatrist in MI5 who specifically asked me if anything like this had happened to me as a kid. In part, I think I've blocked these memories, but writing this feels like the right time to talk openly about my childhood.

I was obviously knocked out for a short period as I woke up in a state of undress, my clothes ripped and my body hurting all over, my neck more than my head. I could see a bible on the floor that was obviously the book used to teach me a lesson, another one. It had bits of my hair stuck in the bindings.

It must have been the sound of the front door closing that brought me round. My mum had come home and she flew into an argument with my dad straight away. I've no idea what was being said, although I do remember her coming into the back room and sharply shouting at me for looking a mess. I'm not sure why she couldn't see what had happened.

As I took myself to bed, piling up my clothes on top to hide underneath and help block the sound of my parents screaming at each other, I still wasn't angry or scared about what had happened. I was determined to not let it happen again. This Sunday I would go to church.

Where was the church? What was church like inside? Maybe it's why the other kids are happy and don't get hit like I do? Because they go to church.

Done deal. As I drifted off under the suffocating heat of the pile on top of me, I tried to count how many *get ups* it would be till I could get to church. I remember I would always call it 'get ups' instead of sleeps. Somehow, sleeping reminded me of dead people. Still, unresponsive, cold. Some part of me even then wanted to see the positive in life, to make the best of a bad situation, but accepted that boys like me had to make sure they weren't seen. That was okay – keeping out of sight gave me breathing space to think about what I was going to do next.

I was almost asleep when I felt a wobbling inside my mouth. Another tooth was loose, towards the back. Reaching in my mouth, I pulled it straight out. It must have been knocked loose when I hit the floor earlier. I held it tight in my fist. There was very little bleeding and, touching the new gap in my teeth with the tip of my tongue, as all kids do, I knew that the tooth fairy would not be visiting this house. She didn't know who I was.

As the days ticked by, I learned to recognize the smell of my dad when he was blind drunk and made sure I was quiet. I would take a tin of beans, a spoon and a cup of water up to my bedroom without being heard. It became like muscle memory, avoiding the squeaking floorboard and remembering how much pressure a door would need to open and close so I could avoid slamming anything. The only problem I had was at night, when I'd always need the toilet. I avoided walking into the firing line of my increasingly violent parents by having a wee on a Spiderman costume a neighbour had given me a couple of years earlier. It was thick, horrible material but seemed to soak up fluid well. It didn't soak up the smell though; my tiny bedroom quickly stank of stale urine. Ironic, really, that twenty years later I would purposely be making sure my clothes stank of piss so I could blend in as someone who was homeless in order to keep eyes on a target.

Finally, Sunday came and I'd made it relatively unscathed apart from red raw legs after my mum found out I'd been using my bedroom as a toilet. All week I'd been asking the other kids at school how to get to the church and avoiding questions about the bruises covering my body. Luckily it turned out that the church was just around the corner from the school itself. I knew that when the little hand on the kitchen clock was at eight and the big hand at the top I had to set off for school, so I would use the same principle to get to church. Hoping I would be able to get there and save myself a week of pain afterwards.

I remember how much quieter the roads were that morning compared to when I walked to school during the week. Also, it felt really strange walking there in my own clothes rather than my school uniform. At the time I didn't appreciate it but I did feel more grown-up. Moving past the school, I repeated to myself the instructions for the church and made it to the front gate. No one was there yet and the door was shut. Moving into the grounds of the church, which were surrounded by old stone walls, I sat on some dry ground underneath a tree and waited. I remember thinking it would make a brilliant Christmas tree, and imagined it full of lights and decorations like everyone else had at Christmas.

Eventually people started to arrive, including the priest and the sisters from my school as well as kids and their parents. I wasn't sure what to do once inside so stayed out of the way, waiting until everyone had gone in and I could hear the muffled sounds of the service starting. Now I felt comfortable enough to enter – my first time ever inside a church, as far as I could remember. I noticed how intricately carved the double wooden doors were as I walked through and under an arch made of huge stones.

Rows and rows of people were all facing towards the far end of the church, listening to the priest read something. I was desperate not to be seen and asked to do something, so I tucked myself away in the back, finding a huge cast iron heating pipe to sit on. It was so warm that after a few minutes I started to drift off, a combination of not sleeping well, coming in from the cold and the monotone rhythmic sound coming from the altar at the front of the church. I only woke when the service had finished and people started to move around, getting ready to leave.

The sudden noise shocked me; panicking, I instinctively ran out before I could be seen and sprinted around the side of the church where the gravestones were. I'm still not sure why I did this, given that I wanted to be there. I could see a couple of the kids from my class walking out with their mum and dad, holding hands and asking to go to the park. The sisters followed afterwards and everyone made their way home or into their cars.

I still didn't know what happened during a visit to the church, but everyone seemed happy. Kids weren't being dragged around, no screaming or shouting from the parents. Strange.

Going to bed that night, warm inside my cave of clothes and blankets, I fell asleep thinking Monday morning assembly would be good because I would be like all the other kids. I would be normal.

The walk to school that Monday was particularly cold, I remember the icy breeze hitting my gums where my missing teeth had left gaps, but I felt good. I was looking forward to school that day.

Sitting in assembly with the children from my class and surrounded, as every Monday, by the nursery children in front of me and the confident older kids behind, I listened to the sister talk about the coming week and tell some story about Jesus. My attention drifted as I noticed the state of my footwear compared to the kids sitting on my row.

All had leather shoes that were clean and not falling apart. My left pump had a mouth where the front of the sole had come away almost completely. But my right pump was the worst. It was split all around the bottom where the rubber had almost completely disintegrated. And I'd only just noticed that they were too small, my toes right at the edge. I was so engrossed in the state of me compared to everyone else, I didn't notice the assembly was standing up.

'MARCUS!' the sister yelled.

You always know you're in trouble as a kid when people shout your surname. Scrambling to my feet, I wasn't sure what I'd missed. Maybe it was time to go back into class. I was smaller than the kids to my left and right and hoped that I would be invisible, despite the sister already shouting my name. Looking for movement, I focused on the gaps between the kids to try and see if anyone was coming for me. Silence apart from the odd sniffle from the nursery kids in front. Suddenly, I was grabbed round the back of my neck, the force of it almost giving me whiplash. It was another sister, who'd come from the back of the assembly hall.

I was dragged backwards and straight to the headmistress's office, where I was dumped into a chair and told to wait. What had I done wrong? The office was small, just room for the head sister's chair and desk, my chair and a small bookcase.

That was it. The sister who was standing guard over me, for whatever reason, left the office briefly.

Even though I was just six years old and smaller than the other kids I was learning fast. Not maths or reading – I couldn't hold my own with my classmates in any of the normal lessons – but I was learning vital skills.

I knew I was about to be hurt. I could sense the atmosphere, I'd been hit before at school, chances were it was going to happen again. Ruler!

Spotting two wooden rulers on the sister's desk, I checked the open door for my guard; still on my own. Sliding off the chair, which was just high enough that my feet couldn't touch the floor, I grabbed both rulers and hid them behind the books on the bookcase. Wriggling back onto my chair, I hoped what I'd done had saved me rather than being about to make my punishment even worse.

Seconds later, both sisters walked in.

'Marcus, why didn't you come to church yesterday?' the head asked in her stern Irish accent. Immediately I looked up, my eyes widening. I can tell her the truth!

'I was, I was there, I went.'

Her voice rose with anger, thinking I'd lied to her. 'Then why, when I asked the children to stand up if they went to church, didn't you stand up?!'

Looking back down, I saw the open-mouthed sole flapping on my pump. It looked sad.

'I did go,' I muttered. 'I fell asleep on the hot pipe.'

Grabbing the underside of my chin, she pushed my head up

so I was forced to look at her. The collar of her blue habit was absolutely pristine white. I guess you can wash the stains out of anything. It didn't matter what I did, these two wouldn't believe me.

As I was shouted at and accused of being a liar and wicked, among other things I didn't really get, the head sister grabbed both my hands and held them in front of me, palms up. Then she turned to her desk, looking confused. *She can't find a ruler! Yes, I'm not going to be hurt today.* I tried my best not to smile or look at the bookcase in case I gave away what I'd done. I was seconds away from freedom, I knew it.

When you're willing to hand out punishments such as hitting a kid with a ruler or washing their mouth out with soap and water, you become quite adept at improvising. I hadn't seen the cane leaning against the desk as a threat because I hadn't seen it being used before. As one sister held my fingers out straight the other one whipped the thin cane into the palm of my hands twice. It was a rapid pain, instantly taking my breath away and making me cry.

As I was escorted from the office to my classroom I was reminded that lying is wicked. There was also something about God's will but I'd zoned out because the pain in the palms of my hands was so intense. As an adult you can shake the pain off but as a young kid you don't have the ability to withstand it. I had learned that I would do anything to avoid more punishment.

I spent the next hour or so being shouted at by the teacher because my handwriting was too scruffy. I couldn't hold the pen properly as little welts started to rise up in perfect straight lines across my palms. I was getting attacked from every angle, even the kids in my class started to join in, telling the teacher that I wasn't holding the pen right or I was still on the first page of the words I had to copy. I needed a way out. A way to stop the sisters thinking I was bad and to make sure I didn't have to do any more work that day, especially writing.

I'd nearly got away with it in the sister's office, but by hiding the rulers I got hit with the cane instead, so I'd made the situation worse for myself. The lesson ended and as the kids headed towards the art room for painting I made sure I was the last one out of the classroom. I didn't want to be seen right at that moment. I would be walking into another firing line as soon as I rounded the corner. I didn't want to be hurt again.

Then I saw the red box on the wall in the corridor and I knew what I was going to do. Every now and again we had a fire alarm test where we all lined up in the playground, and I understood what the box was for. As soon as the hallway was empty, I stood on my tiptoes and pressed the fire alarm hard, pushing the clear plastic into the button underneath. Even though I was expecting it, the instant scream of the sirens in the hallway and the flashing lights made me jump. My heart was pounding as I skipped quickly around the corner to rejoin the kids in my class who were all now walking fast towards the exit, directed by teachers coming out of the various classrooms.

Lining up outside, it was cold and there were constant demands to *ssh* from the teachers as they did a head count of each class. But I was happy. I'd created a situation which had given me some protection; no more shouting or being punished, for now at least.

The kids got excited when the fire engine arrived but the teachers knew this was highly likely to be a false alarm given there was no smoke or fire anywhere. One of the firemen met the head sister and walked into the building. It only took minutes for them to reappear and the teachers to start funnelling us back inside.

Walking past the enormous fireman in his big thick uniform, I saw him smiling at the kids in front of me who were all waving at him excitedly. He turned his attention back to the head sister, not noticing me. I wasn't waving. I was thinking about how I was going to stay invisible in this school. As the sole of my pump slapped open and shut on the cold concrete beneath me I remember thinking to myself, *If you are in trouble, make a big sound somewhere else.* At six years old I would write my letters back to front and miss words while trying to read, my written arithmetic wasn't at the standard of the rest of my class and I didn't understand the purpose of church or God. But I did know how to survive. Not to fight back, but to live another day.

3

STAND AND FIGHT

It was in secondary school that I learned some of the most important skills for any MI5 surveillance operator. I learned how to survive on the streets, to feel confident I could look after myself no matter what. I learned to fight back.

By then I knew my life wasn't the same as all the other kids'. I was underweight, the slowest and weakest in most sports; I didn't go on holidays during half term; and I was in the bottom class for nearly every subject. My mum and dad never came to parents' evenings and I was starting to fall into the habit of living on the streets, sleeping in squats to avoid the carnage at home.

I was old enough to understand that my dad was an alcoholic, a bad drunk. Even though he wasn't a father in any sense of the term, I could see he was haunted by something and that booze was his escape. Unfortunately, it emphasized all his worst characteristics. I was at home enough for my mum and dad not to worry I'd run away but I found solace and learned resilience by keeping out of the way.

I couldn't wait to get out of school. By the time I was

fourteen, I was counting the months until I could join the Army at sixteen and get away. I wanted to belong to something, learn how to fight and protect others, be a part of a family that wanted and needed me there. It couldn't come quick enough.

Other than finding somewhere to sleep and food to eat, I had two problems. The police and paedophiles. There would be regular police patrols looking for signs that boarded-up buildings were being broken into – usually by a melting pot of drug users and gang members. The derelict buildings, from houses to small warehouses, were all privately owned by landlords waiting for the property boom and/or local investment before spending money on renovations, so they boarded the windows and doors up with either steel or heavy woodchip sheets that were instantly used as drawing pads for local spray can owners.

I used to search for a few telltale signs that would indicate whether the derelict building I was looking at was safe enough to sleep in or not. The key thing for me as a small, underfed scruffy fourteen-year-old was the presence of activity. If it looked or sounded like there were people there I would move on. Of course I had to be in fairly close proximity to my school and home – I tried to keep within range of a twenty-minute run.

Parks were normally no good because it is constantly wet in the north. Plus parks and open spaces aren't like they are in posh central London. They are completely open and normally filled with teenagers doing drink and drugs, and gangs looking to take advantage of that.

One night, moving past a boarded-up terraced house, I noticed broken glass under the window frame, empty beer cans and a small mountain of cigarette butts. *Can't sleep in there, too many people lurking in dark places.* Further down this dark street was a warehouse I'd stayed in before. It wasn't really safe for a young teenager, late in the evening, alone, but it was this or be at home. At least out there I was able to control what I did to some extent.

The warehouse was typical of the type of buildings abandoned around there; a huge old mill that became useless over time. Smashed windows, open door, roof partially gone, broken bits of everything scattered around. I squeezed through a gap in the security fencing and quietly moved towards the edge of the building. It was already past my bedtime and I was tired, not to mention hungry, but it looked like I had found a place to curl up. Inside it was dark and stank of piss and cat shit. Horrible. There was just enough light coming in through the broken windows to show a flight of stairs going up one side of a wall.

It was fairly quiet – the lack of cardboard, newspapers or old blankets meant this wasn't a regular sleeping spot – so I squeezed myself underneath the stairs, at the lowest point. Sitting with my back against the wall and with my rucksack, which doubled as my school bag, on my feet to partially hide me, I slowly dropped my head, pulling the hood of my coat up to try and retain some warmth. The staircase gave me shelter from the weather and only left me open on one side. It was a good spot for someone like me.

Jerking awake, I didn't know what time it was. It was still dark. Freezing cold. But the noise of shouting men and women was getting louder. The beam of a torch swung into my part of the warehouse, searching for something. I could see the silhouettes of people against the sky outside – the group was swelling in number. One of them threw a bottle up to the roof and burst into hysterics as it smashed on the floor. Drunk or on drugs. Probably both. Being around people like this had become normal for me but it didn't mean I liked it.

Stay still. Don't move, Tom. I tried to slow my breathing down as the entire group came in, twelve people, mostly guys, three or four girls. Teenagers or older I think, but everyone looked old to me. I was trying to keep an eye on them all while hiding my face, waiting for my chance to make a run for it.

Too late. The beam of the torch caught my eye, which reflected like any other wild animal at night.

'Is that a cat?'

One of the male voices boomed out again: 'Who's that?'

Blinded by the torch, I decided to make a run for it. *Go. Now!*

Grabbing my bag, I sprinted as hard as I could towards my exit, almost instantly getting grabbed, the group closing around me with multiple voices telling me to 'calm down', the odd 'who's this?' My vision was affected by the bright torch which was still intermittently being pointed into my face.

'He's a kid!'

'Please, I want to go.' I didn't like this at all. I was now completely surrounded. The guys looked aggressive, all smoking or drinking, the girls were not much older than me and seemed completely out of it.

'Make him fuck her!' one guy called out.

'Shag her and you can go,' another one said.

I knew what sex was, but I'd never even kissed a girl properly, never mind anything else. I barely knew my own body and my voice hadn't broken yet. Sneaking about in the darkness looking for a safe place to sleep, dealing with the rows and neglect at home and being the invisible loner at school – all that I could cope with because I knew I had only two more years till I could escape. But this situation right here frightened me.

Trying to make another run for it, I was quickly pushed back into the centre of this makeshift prison. One of the guys grabbed a girl in a tracksuit top and leggings with big hoop earrings, pushing her towards me. Her arms instantly went around my neck as if she was getting ready to kiss me, like she knew what was expected of her.

'Shag him, go on Leanne!'

They were like a pack of horny wolves, barking their desires at these girls who were too drunk to care or object. Leanne didn't want to be here either. Even though her eyes were glazed and she was swaying a bit I could feel she hated this. She was like a beaten, broken slave doing everything she was told just to survive another day. *How do I get her out of here while saving my own neck?*

The laughing and shouting around me grew louder as my bag was ripped from my shoulders. It only had a few school books in and a sandwich, all wrapped in a carrier bag to keep them dry. Nothing of any value. I turned, trying to see where the bag had gone, and one of the drunk men gripped my hips and repeatedly forced my pelvis towards the girl, who was still holding her obviously well-drilled position. We weren't the same height and my groin was being forced to bang against her mid-thigh, but it brought me even closer towards this poor girl.

'Stop! I want to go home!'

One of the jeering wolves punched me on the back of my head as someone else tried to pull my trousers down, instantly triggering claws pulling at me from all directions. Swinging my arms out while trying to pull my trousers back up, I knew now I had to fight my way out of this corner. *Don't take the beating, fight!* I'm not sure what happened to Leanne but for a few seconds all I could focus on was surviving.

'Oi!' A voice boomed out of the darkness and as quickly as this gang pounced on me, they ran, disappearing in all directions.

'You OK, young man? I'm a police officer.'

As the male shadow moved towards me I tried to adjust my clothing while scrambling to pick my school books up from the dirty floor.

I really didn't want to be taken home by the police – it would bring even more pain into my world.

Standing up, I came face to face with the policeman who'd saved me just seconds ago.

'Shouldn't you be at home?' he said.

'I'm going now. It's OK. I know the way.'

I was desperate to avoid my mum and dad being introduced to the police. Turning to leave quickly, I knew I would have to stick to the better-lit main roads and run home to avoid the gang of drunk wolves.

'Wait, you've been hurt. Are you OK? I can call a squad car to come and collect you.' The man pulled a walkie-talkie out of his jacket pocket.

'No! I'm fine, don't call anyone. I'm going straight home now, my mum will be expecting me.' She wasn't, but if this policeman thought I had a loving home it was likely he'd just let me go.

Moving close to me as we walked towards the exit, he continued to question me. 'Did you know those guys?'

'No, they just grabbed me. I think one of the girls, called Leanne, was drunk. She looked scared. Maybe you could help her?'

Not being able to do anything for Leanne was already eating away at me; it always will.

'Yes, of course, I'll get my other officers to search the area now. Here, have a drink of water and take this, it will calm you down.'

He produced a plastic bottle of water and a small yellow tablet.

'But I can't swallow tablet medicine . . .?' I started to say, confused. It was true, at that age I still hadn't got the hang of it.

He pushed the tablet towards my face. I closed my mouth and turned my head, trying to move away.

'No, I can't swallow them.'

His fingers ripped into my upper arm. It felt like he was crushing the bone as he pulled me towards him, trying to force the little yellow pill into my mouth, finally showing his true colours.

'Swallow it, you little shit!' he hissed at me.

'No!' I was almost horizontal as I pulled away, my feet scraping on the floor, looking for traction to propel me away from another would-be rapist. In the struggle he must have dropped the tablet but he continued to spit vile insults at me in hushed tones. I distinctly remember I was the only one making a lot of noise. He wasn't a policeman, I knew it now. The more his hands moved over me the more I could smell the same thing I had to deal with at home, alcohol.

He wanted the same thing as the gang. *Got to get away from this right now, otherwise* . . . Well, being fourteen years old I didn't know what was likely to happen. As an adult, looking back, I know. The world is filled with fucking animals preying on those weaker than them.

Your life is filled with defining moments, some good, some horrific. Experiences that shape you for the better and memories that feed the worst parts of your future actions. I made the decision right there and then to fight. I hadn't been able to go to karate lessons or anything like that as a kid, but I knew there had to be a way to beat this guy. I was still shouting and pulling to get away as his stinking hand crawled around my mouth to try and silence me. Suddenly I gained some stability under my feet and, as his body cast a huge shadow over me, I pushed off the floor as hard as I could, driving my head into the lower part of his chest.

He fell backwards but his grip on my top was pulling me down towards him. Instinctively, I stepped forwards and my foot landed on one of his knees. Finally he released me, and as my head lifted and I got ready to run I saw him lying on the floor, the walkie-talkie he was using as a prop on the ground next to him with the battery cover hanging off. His erect penis was already sticking out through the flies of his trousers. I hadn't understood some of the things he had been saying to me – now I knew.

Seeing him start to get up, all the while violently describing what he was going to do to me, was enough to send a surge of pubescent adrenaline coursing round my body. My bag, still unzipped, struggled to stay on my shoulder as I sprinted out of the warehouse, back out the gap in the security fencing and towards home.

No one came after me and I never saw the gang or the rapist posing as a policeman again. Sneaking into the house using the key on a string around my neck, I found it dark and quiet. Obviously my mum had taken an extra shift at work, and because the house didn't smell, I knew my dad was at the pub. Catching sight of the clock in the hallway I saw it was gone eleven at night.

I grabbed two pieces of bread from the kitchen and squirted tomato sauce on them to make a sandwich, then went upstairs to my bedroom.

It was ironic, really, that the only time I felt safe and calm was when I was home alone. I had narrowly avoided something horrendous in that warehouse, but the daft thing was that if I'd stayed at home I would have been OK because my mum and dad weren't in. I'd gotten into a habit of running from danger and becoming blinkered and unable to see the safe zones around me.

I was almost asleep, still dressed, when I realized I was soaking wet and filthy. I was so annoyed I'd finally got to bed only to have to get up and strip off. *Hurry up, Tom*, I thought to myself, *get to sleep, you've got school in the morning*.

It's only looking back on it now that I realize how, even at that young age, people have the ability to compartmentalize horrific situations so they can survive. I never thought about that evening again. Being able to lock memories and feelings away like this isn't a failsafe, though, it's a ticking bomb.

The experience didn't stop me from going back to sleep in squats when things kicked off at home. I'd escaped once and I believed I could do it again. As frightening as it was, if that attack in the squat hadn't happened, I might have become completely broken. It's easy to condition yourself to be constantly abused.

The more you expose yourself to risk, the more resilient

and stronger you become. You know you can't rely on anyone else and you don't need to.

It was not long after I'd escaped being raped that I saw a bloke expose himself to one of the girls from my class on the way to school. Then he grabbed her and pulled her on top of him. She screamed and the other kids nearby just froze, looking for someone to help. I ran after him straight away. Some of the other rougher kids joined in but he was too fast for us.

This protective streak is something I would see a lot with others in the surveillance team who had a similar background to me. We weren't on any kind of noble crusade but we remembered the bad times we'd been through, the fear we felt, and how no one was there for us. If we could make a difference to someone else we would do so.

More than that, I wanted to stop the kind of people who feel they can do what they want to others, because the rules don't apply to them. On a big stage, this is what we did in MI5. I don't care who you are – foreign agents, terrorists – you can't threaten our safety and get away with it. On a smaller stage, my insistence that the rules were for everyone was the reason I ended up working for the security services in the first place.

If you read *Soldier Spy*, you can skip the next bit. I joined the army at sixteen and was on track to become the worst mechanic the Engineers had ever seen when one of our officers took pity on me and sent me on a Physical Training Instructor course instead. I fucking loved it. I took my new role as a PTI very seriously, even making the Commanding Officer take remedial training after he cheated on his sit-ups. I wasn't trying to score points, I just believed that if you're leading 1,500 men you need to be able to do everything you ask them to do. No one is entitled to special treatment just because of who they are. That attitude is why the CO recommended me for Special Operations selection. (Although he might also have been trying to get rid of me!) I passed after six tough months and was one of the youngest people ever to join the army's secretive counter-terrorism unit in Northern Ireland. That was where I met my wife Lucy, who was one of the few women at the time to pass the Special Ops course.

Ian Grey, my handler in Northern Ireland, recruited me into MI5 not long after the 7/7 attacks. I joined A4, part of A Branch, which is the department tasked with surveillance. More specifically, I was part of Green Team. Surveillance is a complex procedure if you don't want to be caught, and by operating in teams we could find and keep control of the target while remaining out of sight. We were trained to blend into our environment, to notice detail and filter what is important and what is not. On the street your life might depend on your ability to read a situation in a fraction of a second.

Being part of a team like this is like no other feeling. In the military you have a special bond with those around you. When I made it into Special Operations, something we know as 'the group', the bond was even stronger. But being in an A4 team was the first time I had complete faith in the people around me, knowing there were no weak links. We never questioned anyone's ability and we all put the operation ahead of ourselves. There was no place for ego. If your target was on his way to the tube with explosives in a backpack, you didn't care about being the one to control him – you handed him over without hesitation if someone else was in a better place. We were driven not to let anyone down – the intelligence officers back at Thames House and especially each other. We knew almost nothing about each other's personal lives and yet we saw each other more than our own families. We lived and breathed surveillance to stop terrorism. With each other. For each other.

4

THE FOLLOW

A couple of days after the terrorist cell was arrested in Wales I was woken up by the sound of my son struggling in his cot. Whenever I was home I would make sure Lucy had as little as possible to do. She was struggling to recover from the birth of our son, which had very nearly killed her. The doctors said the only reason she survived the massive haemorrhage during birth was due to the fact she was so fit. Losing four and a half pints of blood is quite often fatal. I knew she still didn't have enough energy to cope with breastfeeding our humongous baby boy every ninety minutes and do the constant washing newborns bring, never mind keep herself fed too. I wanted to let her sleep through the night, so now I slipped quietly out of bed. I knew what I was getting into as the sound I'd heard is one every parent recognizes – a baby taking a huge shit in their nappy. No problem, I was quite proud of how quickly I could clean him up and put him back down again; I had my own little system going.

'Come here, baba.'

Giving him a big kiss, I thought again how important it was

that I had a good relationship with my son. Having grown up without family care, I was determined to break that cycle.

Unfortunately, the changing table had been moved, so I laid my son down on the bed. I had my baby wipes on my right-hand side, nappy bag at the ready. Controlling his feet lightly but securely, with my left hand I undid his nappy, nice and quick, to be met with the most monstrous shitty nappy I'd ever changed. Because I was kneeling down by the bed it was all at eye level.

'What are we feeding you! Jesus Christ, buddy,' I said under my breath.

I heard a little snigger from Lucy.

'Lucy, have you seen this little guy's nappy? It's like he's been eating mushy peas and curries for a week!'

Almost through cleaning him up, I reached for a fresh wipe just as my son let out the most forceful and loudest fart I've ever heard.

'Fuck . . .'

More laughter from my wife.

'Lucy, if you think that's funny, you'll love this. His fart has just speckled shit all over my face!'

Switching the side light on next to the bed, Lucy saw I was indeed covered in tiny bits of poo.

'At least I had my mouth closed!'

Still laughing, Lucy came to the bottom of the bed, kissed our son to congratulate him and took over so I could wash my face. Just as I checked in the mirror to make sure I'd got it all clean, my work phone started vibrating.

In the mirror I could see Lucy's face drop slightly. I knew she'd been praying for me to leave home on time as planned but this early morning text could only mean one thing. I read the message:

Briefing on air, new job. ASAP

'Fuck me, I'm sorry, I've got to go. Keep your phone next to you, don't worry about doing anything else, just feed yourself and little dude. I'll be home soon.'

Kissing the top of her head, I knew she was putting a brave face on all this.

'Yeah, don't worry, we're gonna have a great day.' She adopted a mock stern expression for the baby. 'But you better not poo on my face or there will be trouble, mister!'

Our son was showered in affection constantly – we often joked about him being the most kissed baby in the world – and it was fucking killing me that MI5 and the country's security was depriving me of the normality I craved.

Driving away from home, I switched the car's radio on and sent a test call to let my team leader know I was on the net.

'Anyone read Charlie Five?'

'*Loud and clear to Team Leader,*' Graeme said. '*We'll wait for everyone else to get on the air, mate, but for now head to the area of Edgware, please.*'

'Roger that.'

It didn't take long before the whole team was on the net and the operations officer gave us a briefing over the air.

'*Morning, Green Team, apologies for the earlier than planned start. This is a briefing for a new job, Operation STARLING.*

59

Following the arrests in Wales, Zero Six recovered a mobile phone at the campsite. That phone has been interrogated by the techs and is confirmed to have belonged to GREEN ATLANTIC. A number of new targets have been identified. To that end, this is a first look at two new targets whose details were on GREEN ATLANTIC's phone. All the details have been uploaded to your Personal Digital Assistants but they are two white cousins, DEEP BLUE and GREEN GARDEN. We need anything you can get to develop a picture on these two – housings, up-to-date photographs, cash cards used, any internet terminals, mobile phones used and GPS'd locations. As I say, refer to your PDAs for more information. I'll pass on an accurate location for them both in a minute. Team Leader back to you.'

'Team Leader roger. Stations head to Edgware and wait for update. We don't have a whole lot of information on the PDAs about the cousins other than their background.'

Traffic at this time in the morning in north London was really light, making progress very quick. I was one of the first cars into the area when Base fired another update on the cousins' location to the team over the radio.

'All stations from Base, be aware DEEP BLUE and GREEN GARDEN have been confirmed into Edgware tube station, both in dark coloured tops, one with blue stripes, no other description available.'

'Team Leader roger that, is anyone close enough to the station to react?'

'Zero Six out on foot towards the station now, searching.'

Ditching my car round the corner, I had to move fast. As I

ran towards the station I was worried by the amount of people getting off one of the local buses outside the entrance and walking en masse towards the tube.

Moving through the station's barriers, I could just make out the backs of the cousins. Losing sight of the targets at this stage would be catastrophic. I followed them onto the platform and then into a carriage that was rammed full of people trying to get to work, parents keeping a tight grip of their children on their way to school, and two terrorists. As we left Edgware southbound on the Northern Line I saw the cousins, who were at the other end of the carriage, refusing to give their seats up to an elderly couple who were struggling to keep their balance.

Two white cousins who grew up in the foster system, recently replacing their addiction to drugs with extremism. I caught glimpses of them through the crowd, signalling to the team on my radio that I had control. I noticed them comparing phones – it looked like they were swapping information they had found, or pictures perhaps. Given how busy this tube was I could get closer and still look natural, but I'd have to wait till the next stop to get off, using the massive rush-hour crowds for cover, and re-enter at the doors next to them. The phone signal on this line was intermittent so I was fairly sure they wouldn't be using the internet, and to get a look at what they were doing on their phones could prove valuable later on.

I knew from their transmissions that the team cars were following this tube on the parallel roads – they were making great progress as they dropped other operators out on foot ready to come and help me out. We still had no idea what these two cousins would do on a normal day.

As the tube lurched slightly, braking as it neared the next stop, I got ready to squeeze myself into the group by the door who would be first to leave. A quick glance over to the cousins showed me that they were preparing to get off too. Getting ready to give a 'stand by' signal on my radio, I took note of the direction of the exit. I had to keep control of these two but in this crowd I was already too far away. *Fuck.*

The tube doors opened and the daily battle of people leaving versus getting on started immediately. Pausing for a second in the doorway of the carriage, using the slight height advantage before I had to step down onto the platform, I saw the cousins already out and walking towards the exit. Shit, this was going to be a scramble. Sending my team the signal that the targets had left the tube, I was praying we would have someone watching the station ready to pick these guys up.

'*Roger the stand by, Zero Six. You've got Eight Nine direct on the outside if you can feed them to me?*'

Still unable to talk with so many people around me, I sent the discreet message to acknowledge I could feed the targets to the exit. I had control of this by the skin of my teeth, only seeing the back of the cousins' heads towards the exit barriers.

'*Eight Nine, roger that. Once they are through the barriers I can take control and I'll clear you out.*'

I didn't get a chance to send a covert reply before Sean took control of the cousins. Situations like this are a surveillance nightmare, with tons of people around and more than one option for the targets once they got off the tube.

'From Eight Nine, I have control. That's DEEP BLUE and GREEN GARDEN OUT OUT and south towards the Alpha Five. Zero Six, you're clear to come out.'

'Roger and Zero Six is backing.'

'Team Leader, roger that. Eight Nine, you have bikes in the area too if you need them.'

So far so good. We had a good pick-up of these two targets, just, and as this was a 'first look' we didn't want any compromises. Passing them around the team was a good idea, but finding that balance of gaining intelligence without getting too close is extremely hard to do sometimes.

'Hold back hold back! DEEP BLUE and GREEN GARDEN have stopped at the junction with the main, looking back on their route. Zero Six can you? I've taken cover.'

By 'can you' Sean was asking if I could take control. It's a shorthand we often used. As I took over I thought, *These fuckers are operationally aware.* This means they aren't just local extremists, it's likely they are planning something too. Luckily I was on the opposite side of the street to Sean, I had plenty of delivery trucks hiding enough of my profile and at this distance I could keep walking with the people in front of me towards the cousins without being obvious. As I whispered into my radio I could see them both moving around, trying to identify anyone they thought was acting suspiciously or they had seen before somewhere else.

'Zero Six has control. No change. DEEP BLUE and GREEN GARDEN continuing to look back on their route. Extremely aware, is anyone ahead to help out?'

'*Yes yes, Bravo Two has eyes on the main if they continue south.*'

'Roger, thank you, and that's both now turning back south towards the main, Zero Six has control.'

'*Zero Six, permission?*'

I knew the team leader would be cutting in soon; he wanted to know why these two were so aware.

'Go ahead. Five-zero metres from the junction with the main.'

'*Thanks. Base from Team Leader, any intelligence on these two, why are they operationally aware?*'

'*Negative, we don't have anything on these two at all yet, other than being seen with previous targets on Operation OWL. This is the first look.*'

I knew the geeks back at Thames House would be doing everything they could to find any intelligence about the cousins but it already felt as if we had started following these men too late. Normally there is a build-up to an attack, little changes in their daily habits until their days are filled with planning.

'Bravo Two from Zero Six. Mate, I need to change my profile. Can you watch the junction while I duck out of view for ten seconds?'

I was fairly sure the cousins wouldn't have seen my face, or at least that they wouldn't be able to remember it, but changing from a T-shirt to a different-coloured hoody would help me stay in their shadow a bit longer without alerting them to the fact the world's best surveillance team were watching their every move. But I barely had time to make the switch, using the high sides of a delivery van to screen my actions, before Bravo Two was back on the net.

'*Bravo Two, all stations. Both targets are IN IN to a Blue Ford Mondeo. VRN Foxtrot Kilo one one Echo Mike Romeo. Vehicle is now SOUTHBOUND SOUTHBOUND at speed.*'

Fuck. These guys were 'dry cleaning' themselves, taking measures to make sure they were free of any surveillance. They were clearly up to something and had a high degree of operational security. We couldn't let them escape – if they went missing now it would be nearly impossible to find them again unless they went to a known address.

Running towards the junction at full tilt, I knew I was in danger of being noticed if someone was providing counter-surveillance for the cousins. In situations like this it becomes a trade-off; you lose some of your operational security to keep control of a target, or you keep your trade craft intact but risk losing complete control of terrorists.

Just as I reached the junction, looking out for a team car to pick me up, a black motorbike appeared from nowhere and skidded to a halt in front of me. It was one of ours, Bravo Two. Ryan passed me a spare helmet from the rear storage box and I slammed it onto my head, no time to fasten the strap. Climbing onto the back, I held onto Ryan and tucked my head down to reduce wind resistance, allowing him to ride and get control of the Mondeo without having to worry too much about me falling off. It had the added benefit of making it impossible to see the world whizzing past at sickening speed.

I could hear the team's transmissions as everyone scrambled to get hold of the cousins as fast as they could.

'Bravo Two is complete with Zero Six, searching for the vehicle now. Update in ten seconds.'

The accelerating force of the bike made me shut my eyes tight and work to control my breathing, repeating in my head: 'calm, calm, calm'. My breath was forced out violently as Ryan rode onto the pavement to get round a truck holding traffic up, and then accelerated off the kerb and back onto the road.

'Bravo Two has control. Vehicle is still southbound on the Alpha Five. Speed six zero, six five miles per hour.'

I love our bikers. Ryan had done me a huge favour picking me up. He was incredibly skilled and I trusted him with my life but at the speeds he was doing as he drove in between trucks and weaved around cars, using pavements to get past awkward traffic, I couldn't help being scared.

'Continuing southbound past the Asda to the offside towards the North Circular. Stations, vehicle isn't hanging around, is anyone else with?'

It was clear from the responses that no one had been able to keep up, and they were all still struggling to get through the heavy traffic.

'*That's a RIGHT RIGHT and westbound on the Alpha four zero zero six.*'

I knew that to keep his cover and prevent the cousins inside the Ford Mondeo from seeing us, Ryan would have to do some manoeuvring. As he pulled on the brakes hard, using another car turning right to hide behind, a manoeuvre we all used from time to time, I could feel his arms lock out against the handle bars to brace against the momentum I was carrying into him. Keeping his voice low, he spoke on the team radio but with a message directly for me.

'*Mate, if they stop and get out I'll dive down a side street and drop you off and try and get ahead to house the vehicle driver. Tap me to acknowledge.*'

Tapping his stomach hard with my fingers, I was praying the cousins would stop soon so I could get off this thing.

'*No change, continuing westbound towards the tube station and the roundabout.*'

'*Team Leader, roger your last Bravo Two. We're still trying to get with.*'

'*All stations that's a STOP STOP STOP, near-side just before the roundabout outside the station, DEEP BLUE and GREEN GARDEN are OUT OUT and on foot.*'

Ryan pulled the clutch of the bike to let the engine revs die right down as he leaned it quickly into a side street to avoid being seen or heard by the cousins. Jumping off, I handed my helmet to him and pulled my hood up, walking back towards the main road we'd just turned off. I couldn't see the car or the targets and I was praying they weren't walking straight towards me.

'Zero Six on foot, checking.'

The traffic was still streaming down on the main road, the station dangerously close. If I didn't get control of them quickly, it was likely they'd disappear onto another tube. Rounding the corner, I managed to catch a glimpse of the vehicle driving off onto the roundabout.

'Bravo Two, for information, vehicle westbound at the roundabout, EXIT TWO, EXIT TWO.'

'*Roger.*'

I could just about hear Ryan's bike on a parallel street moving round to try and follow the vehicle to an address. With these cousins so switched on, we needed to build up the intelligence picture around them, and quick.

'Stations, Zero Six has control of DEEP BLUE and GREEN GARDEN walking westbound towards the roundabout on the north side. If they go into the station can anyone go with?'

I couldn't go onto the tube with them again, it would be operational suicide. Where the fuck was the rest of the team?

'*Charlie Eight One is coming into the area and can deploy if needed.*'

'*Negative Charlie Eight One, I need you for imagery. Stations, anyone else ready for a foot move?*' Graeme said.

The team leader was pissed, it had taken a while for some of the team to wake up and get with it this morning. First looks are generally quite slow, but the behaviour of these two was showing us we had to be on top of our game immediately.

'*You have Four Seven on foot to the north and can go into the station if needed.*'

'Roger that, Four Seven, thanks. Both targets now ten metres, one zero metres, from the station entrance, wait one.'

Quickening my pace, I tried to close the monstrous gap between me and the cousins. Every time a high-sided vehicle or bus went past I lost visual of them.

'Targets continuing WESTBOUND, WESTBOUND,' I said. 'Now past the station. Four Seven, can you ping them through the junction for me at the roundabout while I move up?'

'*Yes yes. I have control, waiting to cross over the roundabout, will give indication on direction when they move.*'

'*Charlie One Two is with this and ready for imagery too.*'

'*Eight Nine is on foot.*'

'*Bravo Two, vehicle housed and address passed to Base.*'

'Roger, thank you. Stations, I want to grip these two now, nice and tight.'

The fact that the targets had not gone into the tube station had given us the vital few seconds we needed to get on top of our game again. Everyone wanted a piece of the follow now. I could feel the hairs on the back of my neck stand up and a cold chill cascade over me. The team was finally all here, backing each other up.

'*From Four Seven, both now walking across the road, continuing westbound, wait one for street name.*'

'You're west on Alexandra Road, next junction is Morpeth Drive. That will be on your right-hand side.'

Vehicle call signs were helping foot crews out perfectly now, using their maps to help us identify compass directions, key points, street names. Now it was starting to come together, it felt like we were unstoppable.

'HOLD BACK HOLD BACK. Stations recip recip, back towards the roundabout.'

When targets start looking behind them and changing direction quickly, or turning back on their route, we call that doing a reciprocal, or 'recip', and it's a clear sign of trying to evade surveillance teams. Luckily the team had found its feet in time to be ready for this sort of behaviour.

'Charlie Nine Four can?'

'All yours.'

'Charlie Nine Four has control, Both DEEP BLUE and GREEN GARDEN now northbound.'

'Stations, any chance of imagery of this?'

'Charlie Nine Four, video is rolling. Got it all. Any foot crew close in case they go into the shop?'

'Four Seven is inside the shop.'

'Roger that, and that's both targets IN IN to the shop on the west side towards you Four Seven, out of sight to me.'

I could see the shop front right on the corner of the roundabout. There was little intelligence to be gained inside – it didn't sell any hardware or mobile phones, or have a post office or currency exchange desk. I waited nearby to support Sharon – Four Seven – while she had control of them inside.

'*All stations, make sure you're ready for a quick move away from here either on foot or vehicle please, all directions to be covered.*'

The team leader was anxious to keep hold of the cousins. Everything we'd seen so far suggested they were in the latter stages of attack planning, we just had no clue what they were about to do or when.

I could hear Sharon whispering into her radio just as I caught sight of both targets. '*OUT OUT, not with.*'

'Zero Six has control, both walking into the car park on the north side of this shop. DEEP BLUE is giving some instructions to GREEN GARDEN near the wall and now taking a picture of GREEN GARDEN on his phone.'

'*Base roger. Thank you.*'

Using a furniture shop for cover, I pretended the overpriced faded leather chair in the window was everything I needed while murmuring into my mic once more.

'From Zero Six, Team Leader, Base – I think this is a recce. DEEP BLUE is moving around GREEN GARDEN and it looks like he's recording film on his phone rather than taking pictures now. It's the TA barracks. Both targets now moving towards the bus stop on the west side, DEEP BLUE is holding his phone unnaturally down by his side, walking past the main gates of the barracks.'

'*I need imagery of this, stations.*'

'*Charlie Nine Four has video and I completely agree with Zero Six, this is a recce!*'

The fuckers are taking video footage and pictures, I thought. This could be one of their targets. The Territorial Army is made up of volunteers and wouldn't have a massive amount of people in the barracks most of the time – there's a reason the TA are nicknamed 'weekend warriors'. That said, it's an easy, soft target for them to hit even when the camp does have part-time troops in place. They wouldn't be as well protected as a normal military base, with battle-hardened troops permanently stationed there.

'*Roger. Thank you. Zero Six, back to you.*'

'Both targets sat at the bus stop on the north side. I can't go with if they get on a bus but I can give them on. Both targets now look like they are taking selfies with their phones from different angles. The barracks is directly behind them.'

'*Roger, thanks. Good work, Zero Six. Can I have a fresh foot crew please, ready to deploy on the bus with them if they decide to board one.*'

Everyone now wanted in on the action. The team felt like a pack of hyenas – we could smell the blood of intelligence and we all wanted a taste. The team leader barely had time to finish his transmission before Aman, Omar and Susan all dived out of their cars and got onto the net to say they were coming close in, ready for a bus move.

'Stations from Zero Six, be aware, if a high-sided vehicle pulls up I will be blocked, so if someone can get into position to give them on then that would be helpful.'

'*Five Nine can and go with.*'

'Great, thanks mate.'

Omar had a great profile. He was mixed race and, because we'd been on Muslim extremists constantly for the past four months, he'd grown his beard out and was wearing a dark grey shalwar kameez – everything you wouldn't expect someone from MI5 to look like.

As a crowd of school children, ushered by their teachers, slowly walked past me, I saw a bus turning off the roundabout towards the stop where the cousins were still taking pictures of the barracks behind them, identifying the cameras located around the front of the camp. DEEP BLUE had spotted the bus and signalled to his cousin that this was theirs.

'Mate, bus approaching, bus approaching,' I said.

'*Five Nine. Have seen and moving towards the stop now ready to go with.*'

'*Team Leader, roger that. All vehicle call signs ready to pick up those left on foot ready to go with this.*'

'*From Five Nine, bus has stopped, both targets are now ON ON, VRN is Mike Echo one four Sierra Victor Foxtrot, it's a number sixteen, ONE SIX.*'

Unable to talk freely anymore, Omar gave the covert radio signal to the team that he had control of both the cousins on the bus. Without the team leader prompting anyone, the vehicle crews swung into action.

'*Charlie Two Six has control, number sixteen double-decker bus with a toothpaste advert on the back is now northbound in slow-moving traffic. I'm three for cover.*'

Knowing how many vehicles are between the car in control and the target vehicle helps everyone assess the risk that control might be lost. If you're eight vehicles back, you've only got control by a thread. And giving the other vehicle crews a visual lock on, like the advert on the back of the bus, was standard practice for us. It was always really helpful, as most wouldn't be able to see the bus number from their positions but could easily see the large smiling man brushing his teeth.

'*Charlie Two Six, Team Leader permission?*'

'*Go ahead Team Leader, no change.*'

'*Base acknowledge this?*'

'*Base acknowledged, and for information, Five Nine has sent a text message through to say the cousins are both speaking in broken Arabic, flicking through pages of the Quran.*'

'*Roger that, thank you. Charlie Two Six, back to you.*'

'*Sorry, Base permission?*'

'*Wait one, Base. Bus has pulled over for a stop on the west side, wait out.*'

I was still near the shop when I spotted Ken driving one of our team cars. He cautiously pulled into the car park to pick me up. I got in, thinking we'd need to create a 'father taking his son out for a drive' type of profile. Ken was the oldest member of the team, and being 900 years old, no one on the streets ever imagined he could be any type of surveillance officer, which was perfect. He wasn't the quickest of drivers but somehow he'd always stay up with the follow, especially in London. He used to work as a London cabby, and clearly had never forgotten his 'knowledge' test. Today was no exception.

'*Stand by signal heard from Five Nine, and have seen, that's DEEP BLUE and GREEN GARDEN now OFF OFF the bus and walking directly towards the park area, walking south, page sixty-two of your map books.'*

'Ken, drop me off here, mate. I'll go into the park from the south end. Have you got a football in the boot?'

'Of course.' He seemed surprised I'd even asked.

'Roger that, anyone keep control of this?'

'Six Two on foot. I've got control, both walking slowly into the park now.'

'Nine Eight is backing.'

'One Four is supporting to the west.'

'Charlie Three Three has imagery going.'

'Seven Two is supporting to the east.'

'Zero Six has the south of the park.'

'Excellent work, stations. Six Two, all yours.'

This looked like a classic anti-surveillance move here, trying to draw us through busy areas, onto different modes of transport, straight into wide-open spaces with little cover. It makes it easier to spot if anyone is one your trail. Luckily our team was all over this and the team leader had very little to do.

'From Six Two, both walking south on the eastern path of the park. They seem to be purposely trying to use the cover of the trees. Stations, be aware they are extremely vigilant, looking at everyone around them.'

'From Team Leader, give them loads of room here.'

'Charlie Three Three, can control this if you like? I have video too.'

'Six Two, great, thanks mate, and backing.'

It was clear the cousins were extremely paranoid, again another massive indicator that they were a fair way along in their attack planning.

'*From Charlie Three Three, both DEEP BLUE and GREEN GARDEN now at the fork of the eastern path and taking a right right and west through the park. For information, this is in the middle of park.*'

As I kicked the ball around, trying to flick it up off the grass, I could see the cousins about 150 metres away. There were other people in this park – dog walkers, runners, couples with push chairs, even a homeless guy – and that helped our cover. If these two were studying everyone in the park they would have a lot to remember. Turning away from them, I decided I needed to try and blend in a bit more. It looked like I was waiting for my mates to turn up for a kick about, but it would be better if I managed to integrate myself with a group of teenagers nearby, who were passing a ball around aimlessly.

'*Zero Six, be advised that's DEEP BLUE and GREEN GAR-DEN now taking the left path at the end on the west side of the park and walking south towards your position, one hundred metres away. They could be doing figure of eights around the park.*'

I had to act quickly. The cousins were too aware for my liking and if the team left things down to chance we'd fuck this job up before we'd managed to find out what was going on. Purposely mis-kicking my ball towards the teenagers, I ran over and, as they flicked the ball back to me, I volleyed it straight back over to them. Thankfully they were a bit bored and didn't seem to think I was too much of a weirdo when I asked to join their game till my mates arrived. I threw myself into it with a fake smile – I hated football, but these five teenagers were my new assets and I needed them to play their role perfectly, without them knowing it.

Just as we were getting into the swing of it, I heard Charlie Three Three come back on the net giving me a countdown.

'*Zero Six for information they are two zero metres from your position now, still extremely alert although no interest in you so far.*'

I had to engineer a bit more cover as they walked past and thankfully one of my new assets used too much force when he kicked the ball over to me, allowing me to miss it completely and let it fly past my head away from the path. Turning round to jog after the ball, I now had my back towards the cousins as they drew adjacent to my fellow footballers.

Labouring my jog as if I was too tired to run properly I gave the cousins as much time as possible to get past the group of teenagers before I had to return.

Bending down to pick the ball up, I got a quick upside down view of the cousins walking past the group, showing no interest at all. Returning with the ball, I could see the cousins were now away from me, continuing their loop around the park. I needed to break away from this small group so I didn't overstay my welcome. Faking a phone call, I made my excuses and moved to the south-west corner of the park.

We'd been on this follow for some time now but everyone was still sharp. All of us had the ability to keep going for many hours without getting mental fatigue, losing focus or getting distracted. With a job like ours, there was no choice.

'Team Leader from Charlie Three Three, both targets extremely paranoid but I don't think there is any intelligence to be gained by having people on foot inside the park now. Continuing north on the east side back towards the middle of the park.'

'Roger that, Charlie Three Three. Quick question, have you got uninterrupted video of these two?'

'Yes.'

'Great work, all foot crews withdraw out of the park and into a vehicle call sign please. Stay close in to react.'

'Base permission?'

The transmissions on the radio were absolutely constant now.

'Go ahead,' Charlie Three Three said. *'Targets continuing north on the eastern path of the park.'*

'Thank you. Team Leader and stations, background checks on the cousins have shown they are likely to be dealing drugs as a way of financing themselves. Intelligence from G Branch is suggesting they might be using a makeshift mosque in Edgware. Can we take on any new contacts, please?'

As the team leader acknowledged the new tasking, to follow anyone these cousins made contact with, the transmissions were handed back to Charlie Three Three, who now had both of them heading towards the top corner of the park again.

Almost out of the park, I had to try and find someone in the team to come and pick me up, but I could hear the updates from Charlie Three Three speeding up.

'*Both targets in the area of the exit to the park and the main, stations be aware that they aren't acting normally here, it looks like they are about to run, lots of looking around them.*'

'*Team Leader, roger.*'

No one else acknowledged – we knew if we all started to reply it would make it impossible for Charlie Three Three to give us a warning that the cousins were trying to escape whatever was making them paranoid.

'*STATIONS! That's DEEP BLUE and GREEN GARDEN now sprinting SOUTH SOUTH down the park, I need someone to take control if they make it out of the park.*'

'Zero Six has the bottom of the park to the south-west.'

Fuck, I had already been close to these two, now they were sprinting in my direction. I could either front this out or try and get into a more covert position, but if I did that I ran the risk of acting oddly and giving the cousins the evidence they needed to confirm their paranoia. Where is the weak point in this surveillance follow? The park was easy to contain and we could watch everything they did; if they made it onto the main road they could be picked up by a vehicle, or they could get a bus or taxi. I knew what I had to do, I just didn't quite know how to do it yet.

'*From Charlie Three Three, that's both targets now across the park to the south-west exit, still sprinting. Two hundred metres away now.*'

'Zero Six roger.'

They were getting closer. I had to get out of this park to get control of them both as they left. Fucking hell, I needed cover.

As I left the park I couldn't see any shops, cafes or pubs I could go into.

'*From Charlie Three Three, that's one hundred from you, Zero Six.*'

'Roger, let them run to me.'

I was committed now. The team was depending on me and I could tell by the lack of transmissions from any of the vehicle call signs there was no one else covering this exit. There was nothing close by to let me live my cover without the cousins seeing me. A motorbike was parked up thirty metres up the street. This was so fucking risky I couldn't believe I was even considering it, but I had no choice, the gamble needed to be taken.

'*Three zero metres to you Zero Six, still running fast.*'

'Zero Six has direct on the exit, wait out.'

Walking up to the motorbike, a brand new Yamaha R1, I knew I could soon be facing the unhappy owner, who presumably lived in the house it was parked outside. I sat on the bike and angled the offside mirror to point at the park exit behind my right shoulder.

'Zero Six has control. Both OUT OUT of the park and now WALKING directly south over the road. Anyone else close in?'

'*You have Charlie Two Seven in the area, give us thirty seconds, mate.*'

Very aware I had just climbed onto an expensive bike I didn't own, but still needing to live my cover in case anyone was watching me, I pretended to inspect the condition, as if I was a potential buyer. I gave one last look in the mirror: no sign of the cousins at this angle. Jumping off, I moved to the front of the bike to enable me to look back towards the cousins' likely position.

'Still continuing to walk south now on the opposite side of the road. Now stood static looking directly back at the park exit.'

'Team Leader, roger that. Base acknowledge still very aware.'

'Base roger.'

'Oi! That's my fucking bike!'

Shit. The owner of the bike came barrelling out of his house. He wasn't massive but I knew he wanted to kick my head over the other side of the street. My cover needed to stay intact.

'Hi, mate,' I said, holding out my hand. 'I'm John. I rang about the R1 an hour ago. You're Bryan, right? Looks good, different colour though . . .?'

'What?' I'd stopped him in his tracks but he was still glaring at me. I might have defused the situation but having momentarily seized the advantage I had to keep this story going.

'Sorry about jumping on before knocking on the door for you, but I've been to see a few now and you wouldn't believe the amount of dodgy adverts trying to rip people off. Any problems with it? Looks clean and straight, not been dropped, has it?'

'I'm not selling it . . . my name's Andy. What are you talking about?'

'I'm sure this is the place, look, I found you on Autotrader . . .'

I took my iPhone out of my pocket, still playing dumb but working in an exit strategy.

'Look mate, it's here . . . wait a minute, I don't have a great signal here . . . this is Ringwood Way, isn't it?'

'No mate, that's not round here.'

'How the fuck did I end up here then? Listen, sorry, was it Andrew?'

'Andy.'

'Sorry, Andy, mate, I'm really sorry, I'm in the wrong place. Don't suppose you're selling this one are you?'

When a proud smile spread across his face I knew I'd won him over. 'Sorry, no, I'd never sell it.'

'Don't blame you, she's stunning.'

Running my hand over the tank and down the seat, I made my getaway cleanly.

'Sorry again, mate. I've got to try and find this bike now before I have to get back to work!'

'No worries, good luck.'

I heard Andy close his house door behind me as one of the vehicle call signs offered help controlling the cousins.

'*Zero Six, Charlie Nine Seven can?*'

'All yours,' I said. 'I'm local if you need foot support.'

'*Base permission?*'

'*Go ahead,*' Charlie Nine Seven said. '*No change, both targets still static on Copeland Gardens at the junction of Warren Road looking north-east.*'

'*Stations, latest intelligence suggests they are waiting to be let into an address on Copeland Gardens to stay the night. Once housed we're happy for you to withdraw.'*

'Team Leader, roger. Zero Six close in to help ID the house, assisting Charlie Nine Seven.'

'Zero Six, roger.'

Moving closer to the junction, using the cars parked along the street for cover, I could see the cousins clearly waiting for someone. Obviously they had run out of the park to try and get into the house without being seen, which made this address a key part of the operation now. But if the operations officer at base was telling us to pull off then they had good reason to.

'From Charlie Nine Seven, that's both DEEP BLUE and GREEN GARDEN IN IN to an address on Copeland Gardens. Zero Six, for your information it's the one with the dark brown door with the black guttering.'

'Yeah, have seen, wait one while I confirm house number.'

There was absolutely no point in blowing my cover getting close up to the door. I'd be able to see the house if I stayed on this junction and walked towards Copeland Gardens then past it and away from the address. I wouldn't even need to be on the same side of the road as the house.

Getting to the end of the road, I could see the house the cousins went into directly opposite the T-junction.

'SEVEN EIGHT, number SEVEN EIGHT Copeland Gardens.'

'Charlie Nine Seven, yeah, that's the right one, Zero Six.'

'Team Leader, everyone cease and withdraw back to base. Good work guys, acknowledge down the list.'

We weren't handing over control to another team, so these two cousins would be on their own for the next few hours. I didn't like that. In reality, operators like me had no fucking choice – we are given targets to hunt down and we do it. But it didn't stop us feeling like our pack of hyenas had left too much meat on the bone for one day.

Walking away from the house the cousins had entered only a minute ago, I saw Fatima in Charlie Nine Seven drive past me and take the next turning. There was no need to sort logistics like this out on the net; everyone knew I needed transport back to north London to pick my car up before getting into Thames House for debriefing.

Rounding the corner, I saw Charlie Nine Seven, nice and discreet.

'Thanks mate,' I said, getting into the passenger side.

'No dramas, near Edgware Station, isn't it?'

'Yeah, mate. I hate leaving jobs like this, they probably won't come out again but if they do we'll miss it all.'

'I know, me too, just hope we get a decent update from the ops officers.'

Fatima shared my frustration but she was right, we'd have to wait until the debrief to find out why we'd been pulled off now. Once we made it back to my car I let Fatima go on ahead, so we didn't end up travelling to Thames House in convoy. I was about twenty minutes behind the rest of the team, who were sitting in the briefing room ready to start picking the operation apart when I arrived.

'Great,' the briefing officer said, seeing me walk in. 'Listen in then Green Team, I'll start the debrief.'

Bollocks. Because I was the last one in I couldn't sit at the back of the room – the rest of the team had already had that idea. Now I'd have to sit near the front with the team leader. Smiles instantly filled the faces of my fellow operators as they all knew I'd feel like I was back at school, sitting next to the teacher. Plus, having people sitting behind you is something we always try to avoid. Even in a safe environment it feels uncomfortable. Looking towards the back seats, I let my feelings be known.

'Fucking pricks.'

My little muttered comment made the team laugh but caused the briefing officer to raise his voice in order to keep control.

'Come here, Tom, let's hold hands!' the team leader said, patting the seat next to him. He knew we needed to decompress. The team had been working hard today and although we didn't want any thanks or medals for what we did, it was nice to know we were appreciated.

The briefing officer raised a smile at my new intimate relationship with the team leader before quickly going on to explain why we'd pulled off from the cousins once they entered the address on Copeland Gardens.

'The house they entered is a known drugs den. It seems the cousins are relapsing. The paranoia you witnessed today may well have been caused by their addiction. However, treat it as you always would, don't take chances.'

I'd seen a lot of addicts over the years, grew up with it all around me, and their behaviour didn't seem like they were desperate for a fix.

'At this stage of the operation we don't want them to ping you when it appears they are just sleeping in a drugs den. We're monitoring chatter about potential military attacks based on them taking photographs outside the barracks.'

The team leader let go of my hand. He needed to voice his opinion, no more jokes.

'It's clear to the team these two are in attack-planning mode. Maybe the electronic intelligence isn't supporting that, but what we are seeing on the ground is that these two need to be watched constantly.'

The briefing officer was not persuaded, he'd already made his mind up.

'No one is doubting what you have all seen and we are factoring that into the operational planning. It's likely you'll be deploying on them again in the morning, but let's get you home and I'll see you back here at zero five thirty hours.'

As soon as the team heard the words 'get you home' we all bolted out of the briefing room, desperate to see our wives, husbands, children, dogs, cats or catch the latest episode of *Game of Thrones*.

Anything that would help us switch our focus to something relatively normal. The team leader stayed behind to have it out with the briefing officer, to make sure he knew how our team felt about these two. They weren't normal drug addicts who just happened to have converted to Islam; we needed to take them seriously. The electronic intelligence we had on them wasn't matching the high degree of operational reconnaissance and anti-surveillance being employed.

On my long drive home, despite being knackered from a full day of surveillance, I couldn't stop thinking about the cousins and what they were doing at this exact moment. Had they left that drugs den and gone to recce more places to attack? Drugs dens are normally easy places to find guns too – was that the real reason they had gone there?

As much as I wanted to be with Lucy and our son, a part of me didn't want to go home and relax, watching *X Factor* or some other reality TV shit, because that wasn't my reality. My world was right now, and all it had ever been was tracking down those who want to kill people and making sure they were punished.

5

OPERATION STARLING

Walking into the briefing room, I could see some of my team already downloading the fresh intelligence gained overnight on the two cousins. I was hoping we'd get a grip of them quickly once we were out on the ground. As the briefing officer walked in, I saw that he looked tired, like he'd been up all night. His eyes were bloodshot and his shirt wasn't tucked in as it normally was. The fact he'd asked the team leader to assemble us ready for an immediate briefing confirmed the operation was moving fast.

'Green Team, apologies for the slightly early briefing on Operation STARLING, but you need to get on the ground quickly. Please take a moment to sync your watches. G Branch have been feeding in intelligence on DEEP BLUE and GREEN GARDEN, the cousins you followed yesterday.'

The team leader's conversation with the briefing officer last night had obviously had the desired effect, but the agent handlers of G Branch wouldn't have been able to recruit the cousins yet. Maybe they had someone close to them. Looking around at my team, I saw some of them lean in as the briefing officer continued.

'I have been dealing with G Branch throughout the night, who have said the cousins have become close to a local businessman they met at their current mosque. A completely clean skin. However, his daughter was killed in a British airstrike in Iraq, while she was visiting her new husband's family.'

Fucking hell, it was the perfect motivation to hate Britain. Those members of my team who were leaning in, listening intently, now hung their heads. Sometimes it feels as if we are fighting on a merry-go-round. We try and prevent extremism, but when we do stupid shit like killing civilians, how the hell does anyone expect terrorism to stop?

'We have no actionable electronic intelligence on this man at the moment. However, G Branch believe it's worth having a look at him, so today you'll be deploying out to the address on the screen and your PDAs. The target has been given the codename MAROON OTTER. Today's objectives are: up-to-date photographs and house any contacts made. His office address is also on your PDAs and he's expected to be there today.'

Switching on my PDA, I entered the encryption key to unlock all the target information, addresses, known contacts, photographs, vehicles – absolutely everything that could help us operators on the ground do our job better is loaded onto these little devices. The problem was, we had a passport image and a few addresses, that was it. MAROON OTTER really was a clean skin, a complete unknown.

Just before we started to discuss tactics with the team leader, the briefing officer left us with one final point.

'Team, after various briefings and updates with different departments and your team leader over the past eight hours or so, be mindful how the cousins were acting yesterday. It's highly likely they are going to do something serious soon. If MAROON OTTER is involved in any way, we need to stop him, and quick.'

We'd done hundreds of operations like this before, but something about this one had got the senior intelligence officers worried. We accepted it was need to know, and we might never find out what was going on behind the scenes. People panicking over this particular job didn't affect our team anyway. Every target was the same; we hunted them down and controlled their lives. It was always that simple. It had to be.

The team leader made sure we were going to be on top of our game straight away this morning.

'Right, grab your kit, channel six. We'll organize positions out on the ground, we need to get out there.'

As the whole team rushed down to the garage, you could feel the sense of urgency everyone had, no chat or banter between any of us. We all drove out the barriers and headed across Lambeth Bridge ready to go and get MAROON OTTER. Every team car was being driven with total purpose to get up to High Wycombe quickly. We wanted this guy.

'All stations, shout up for test calls.'

Waiting for my turn to respond, I followed Mike in the car

in front, who was making good use of the bus lanes to get around all the traffic.

'Charlie Eight is on,' I said.

'Roger, thank you, close in to the office address. See if you can identify any vehicles.'

'Roger that.'

'Bravo Two is on channel six.'

'Great, thanks Bravo Two. Can you hold out of the area to react on a stand by for a vehicle move?'

'Yes yes.'

'Stations, that's everyone on channel six now. Once Charlie Eight gets close in can we plot up on all the routes around him to react to a vehicle or foot move please.'

This was how we would normally surround a target: by 'plotting up' around an address or a location where we know the target is, covering all the routes in and out to make sure we see everything and, more importantly, can react quickly if we need to.

It didn't take me long to make it to MAROON OTTER's home town. 'Charlie Eight, in the area now. Checking for vehicles.'

'Thanks Charlie Eight, stations listen for positions please.'

'Bravo Two, can you go to the north, there is a Tesco which will give you fast access to the North Circular.'

'Bravo Two, yeah, in position here already.'

'Thanks. Can I have Charlie Six Six close in to support Charlie Eight.'

'*Charlie Six Six, roger that. Charlie Eight, I'm just south-east of you on Princess Way.*'

'Roger that mate, cheers.'

'*Anyone give Bravo Five a test call?*'

'*Loud and clear, Bravo Five, thanks for joining last minute. Can you wait north near the North Circular too please, to react with Bravo Two. There is an Ikea slightly north.*'

'*Roger that.*'

The North Circular could prove a problem if the target decided to leave quickly, so having two bikers on this job was awesome. They had the ability to keep up with fast-moving cars without standing out too much.

Parking up in the office car park, I made sure the front of my car faced directly into a wall, making me harder to spot for anyone walking past. Using my mirrors, I tried to identify the registration plates of the other cars, but it was mega busy and in order to maintain my cover I had to compromise on how much I could actually see. I figured I had a bit of time though.

'*Charlie Nine Zero, are you in the area yet?*' Graeme asked.

'*Yes yes, where do you want me?*'

'*Great, can you wait north in McDonalds please, ready to react on a stand by or a drive past if we need something checking?*'

'*Roger that.*'

I'd checked seven cars so far and nothing was coming up as a known vehicle. I angled the electric mirror on my right further out and up to get the last registration number. I could only make out the last letter, T, the rest being blocked by the vehicle next to me. Getting out of the car to check would look shit and immediately draw attention. Giving myself a minute, I rechecked the PDA to see if this dark blue Honda Civic was on the list of hundreds of cars potentially associated. It was a long shot but there was a blue Honda Civic listed, with the last letter of the VRN being a T. I needed help.

'Team Leader, do you read Charlie Eight?'

'Go ahead.'

'I've checked all the vehicles in the car park, only one possible but I can't get the full VRN. I can stay in position with direct on the front door of the office to give a stand by for MAROON OTTER if someone can check the VRN of a dark blue Honda Civic for me? Last letter of the VRN is Tango.'

The team leader didn't get a chance to respond before Mark got on the net offering his help: *'Charlie Nine Zero will check that.'*

'Roger, thanks Charlie Nine Zero. Stations, Charlie Eight has direct on the exit/entrance to the office, everyone else is plotted up. Let's wait and see if MAROON OTTER comes out. Be mindful of other targets coming into the area please.'

'Charlie Nine Zero, roger, two minutes, Charlie Eight.'

'Roger, thanks mate. For your information, as you drive into the car park it's nosey parked facing the entrance to the right.'

'Thanks, mate.'

I'd probably just about be able to live my cover in this car park for an hour or two if I stayed still, but the moment I got out and returned to my car having gone absolutely nowhere I'd raise people's awareness of me. And it's always the third party that's likely to kill you, not the actual target.

Mark immediately got on the net.

'Charlie Nine Zero, VRN confirmed Papa Uniform five seven Uniform Uniform Tango. On the PDA this is HARBOUR FISH's car from Operation GULL.'

Mark had obviously checked the details of the Honda on his PDA himself as he drove round to the car park, in case the VRNs did match, rather than just noting the VRN for Base. It's little things like this, marginal time savings, that make the difference.

'Base, roger.'

The speed at which the operations centre replied let us all know they were checking if this was just a coincidence or if HARBOUR FISH – a target from another recent operation – was involved in in some way. I was quite happy and settled in this car park waiting for MAROON OTTER to appear. Reaching down into the door pocket, I pulled the PDA out again, seeing if I had an up-to-date picture of HAR-BOUR FISH in case he came back to his car. I was just in time.

The sun glared off the front door of the building as it swung open. A male walked out, talking on his phone.

'STAND BY STAND BY. That's HARBOUR FISH OUT OUT of the office main door and towards his vehicle, the blue Civic, wearing a green baseball cap and white top. He's solo.'

'Charlie Six Six can go with this if you want?'

'Yes yes, Base acknowledge please.'

'Roger that. Team Leader, we'd like you to split and remain on MAROON OTTER too please.'

'Wait one, stations, please. From Charlie Eight, that's HARBOUR FISH into his vehicle, vehicle is reversing and towards the exit. Now out of sight to me towards you CHARLIE SIX SIX, he's moving quick.'

'Charlie Six Six, roger and have seen. I have control of HARBOUR FISH, vehicle is one up, and now northbound on Bradbury Road held at red, pole position showing a nearside indication at the junction of the North Circular.'

'Roger, stay on this channel please, Charlie Six Six, unless we see MAROON OTTER. Base, can we have a spare channel for Charlie Six Six if we need it.'

'Channel seven for HARBOUR FISH if you see MAROON OTTER.'

'From Charlie Six Six, HARBOUR FISH has jumped the red lights and is now westbound on the north circular.'

This guy was clearly in a rush. We still didn't know if he'd met MAROON OTTER operationally or if all this was a coincidence. I was just glad at this stage that I'd noticed the car in the first place.

'HARBOUR FISH's vehicle continuing west on the North Circular, speed now six five, seven zero miles per hour.'

'Roger that, Bravo Five is backing and can if he keeps increasing his speed.'

'Great thanks mate, can you now?'

'*Moving up now, can see the vehicle in the distance. For information, HARBOUR FISH's vehicle has a brake light out on the offside.*'

Having little visual indicators like a faulty brake light can mean an easy lock-on for anyone trying to get with the follow.

'*Bravo Five has control, vehicle is now alongside the area of the Ace Cafe to his offside, speed eight five, nine zero miles per hour on the North Circular westbound.*'

HARBOUR FISH was clearly in a rush. Whether he was trying to get somewhere or get away from someone, we still didn't know, but the transmissions were constant. Then I caught the door of the office building opening again. This was going to be a busy day.

'STAND BY STAND BY, MAROON OTTER is OUT OUT of the office block and towards the car park.'

'*Bravo Five, roger, switching to channel seven.*'

'*Charlie Six Six, roger.*'

'*Base, roger.*'

'From Charlie Eight, MAROON OTTER is wearing a white shirt, black trousers, black shoes. Continuing out of the car park on foot. I can't go with.'

I knew the team leader would now have both channels on in his car, listening to Bravo Five and Charlie Six Six, who'd taken on HARBOUR FISH, tearing around the North Circular, while at the same time listening to the rest of us with MAROON OTTER.

'*Stations from Team Leader, I'm joining the HARBOUR FISH follow. I have both channels on, Base acknowledge.*'

'*Roger that.*'

We needed to get hold of MAROON OTTER quick, and there was too much admin being sorted out on the net when all that mattered at this exact moment was getting hold of our target.

'WAIT OUT, MAROON OTTER is out of sight to Charlie Eight, last seen towards Princess Way!'

I was being a bit arsey on the net here, but I didn't want us to miss a whole day's surveillance on the target because of bad discipline on the radios.

'*Yeah, Zero Four has control of MAROON OTTER, walking north now on the east side of Bradbury Road.*'

Sarah, who was Zero Four, had moved in to the close in position when we took on HARBOUR FISH. I had to stay where I was, though. If I left the car to back Sarah on the foot follow, it would be obvious we were interested in MAROON OTTER. She was an incredibly hard-working operator. Surveillance didn't come naturally to her but over the years she had developed the ability to see when our team had left a spot open that could potentially let a target slip through.

'*Five Nine backing.*'

'*Six Eight is ahead with eyes on the North Circular junction.*'

Everyone was fighting to get hold of MAROON OTTER. We all knew we had to work that much harder and smarter because the follow on HARBOUR FISH had reduced our team size by three vehicles.

'*Roger the backing,*' Sarah said. '*Six Eight, he's walking towards the traffic lights, can you and let me know direction?*'

'*Yes yes, Six Eight has control, looking to cross over at the pedestrian crossing on the east side.*'

Sarah would be getting into some cover to avoid being seen by MAROON OTTER at this busy road crossing. It's natural to look both ways when you cross the road. The last thing we want as operators is to be caught in the eye line of anyone taking a look around them.

'*From Six Eight, that's MAROON OTTER now walking across the North Circular to the north and towards McDonalds.*'

'*Zero Four, roger and backing.*'

I needed to get out of this car park. MAROON OTTER and HARBOUR FISH hadn't seen me hiding but it was pointless leaving it to chance if they came back. I knew the team leader would be up to his eyes in two different follows, I had to speak to Base on the phone.

'Hello, can I help you?'

Standard opening line, never giving away names or what type of organization the phone number was connected to.

'Alex, its Zero Six. Mate, have you got anyone monitoring the cameras?'

'Yes, we do,' our operations officer said. 'What do you need?'

'I'm going to switch the camera on in Charlie Eight and angle it towards the work address entrance for MAROON OTTER so I can get in on this foot follow.'

'Switch it on and we'll watch for good feed.'

Leaving my car there, with the covert camera giving the

operations centre a live feed of the building, was the best way of splitting our assets. It would allow me to get out of the car park and on the foot follow while retaining a constant feed on MAROON OTTER's work address. Using the small remote control, I angled the camera towards the rough area of the door, the quiet dull groan of the motors moving the camera lens giving me the reassurance that this would work.

'How's that picture?'

'Yeah, we have picture, can you zoom in tighter please? We'll only get the back of him if he returns to work but it would be nice to have a clear facial image of anyone coming out.'

'Yeah, roger that, how's that?' I gave the slightest of touches on the remote to zoom in.

'Perfect, Zero Six.'

'Great, what I'll do now is switch the camera to remote so you can control it from there if you need to.'

'Roger, thank you.'

Hiding the remote control away and switching my personal radio on, I quietly got out of the car, locking it manually to avoid the four-way flashes 'lock' buttons set off, and walked out of the car park. As soon as I was onto the main road walking north, I put my hood up and morphed into the environment. If you don't want to stand out, you match your speed and posture to others around you. In a dodgy area, you might slope along, hands in your pockets. In the City you would be suited and booted, walking quickly with purpose. Today I walked with the slightly hunched-up look of a bloke on the way to the Job Centre. I could see Sarah up in front.

She still had control, and using her as a guide I tried to see MAROON OTTER in the distance but there was way too much traffic.

'*Zero Four from Six Eight, for information he's into the area of the McDonalds on the north side now, I can give him in if you want to go with?*'

'*Zero Four, roger.*'

'*Sarah, that's him in now, IN IN to McDonalds north side of the North Circular. Crews, for information, this is on the junction of Saint Raphael's Way, north side of the North Circular, page eighty-six in your map books.*'

'*Base, roger.*'

'*Team Leader, roger. Crews, for information, we have HAR-BOUR FISH under control in the area of RAF Northolt on the Alpha four zero, west of your position.*'

'*Zero Four, roger that. This McDonalds is busy so I'm going to go straight in.*'

It didn't take long before Sarah gave us the signal over the radio that she had control of MAROON OTTER inside the McDonalds. Rebecca gave the acknowledgement that we'd all heard her control signal outside.

I knew Sarah would be trying to get covert video footage of MAROON OTTER inside. It was a waiting game for the rest of the team outside.

'*Stations from Base, we have the cousins from yesterday DEEP BLUE and GREEN GARDEN into the office.*'

When you've been in this world for as long as I had, you know when seeing multiple targets in the same area is just a coincidence and when it's all clearly linked. HARBOUR FISH, MAROON OTTER and now DEEP BLUE and GREEN GARDEN had all been seen going through the same door within a couple of hours.

'*Team Leader, roger that, crews stay on MAROON OTTER.*'

As Sarah acknowledged the previous messages from inside McDonalds, Base sent a further update.

'*From Base, White Team is deploying now to take on the cousins.*'

Base had been constantly updating the intelligence officers on the desk in Thames House as this operation unfolded, and clearly they wanted a tight grip on all the players in this job.

'*Stations from Base, be aware that's DEEP BLUE and GREEN GARDEN OUT OUT, on foot, both dressed in dark clothing.*'

Multiple targets running around in a small area, an MI5 surveillance team on the ground and a second one rushing to the scene, all while people went about their daily lives none the wiser. I loved it. You could be walking your kids to school or nipping to the shop for some milk and not realize you're surrounded by terrorists and MI5.

Sarah sent another covert signal on the radios to acknowledge that the cousins were back out in the open. A good twenty minutes went by before I caught sight of them both walking over to our position north of the office.

Even though White Team were obviously here to control the cousins, we had to keep a loose eye on them too in case they met up with MAROON OTTER. There were now more MI5 operators in this area than normal civilians going about their daily lives! I had to be careful because I'd been so close to the cousins yesterday in completely different settings, first on the tube then playing football in the park.

'*STAND BY STAND BY from Six Eight, that's MAROON OTTER OUT OUT walking towards the main now, Base acknowledge.*'

'*Base roger and White Team informed.*'

'Zero Six roger and I have control, MAROON OTTER waiting to cross over the North Circular outside McDonalds, very relaxed, no looks back. Is there anyone south I can let him run to?'

'*Yeah mate, Nine Four is south and can give him back towards the office.*'

'Cheers Nine Four, that's MAROON OTTER now making his way through the traffic south across the North Circular, towards you.'

We were passing the target around the team; there was no sense in all of us moving from our positions, especially now White Team were here and the cousins were in the open. Remaining still and living our cover was the perfect thing to do in this situation.

'*Nine Four has control, MAROON OTTER is still walking south, now on Bradbury Road on the west side, looking to cross.*'

'*Nine Four from Base, we have picture of the work address, you can let him run if he goes towards.*'

'*Roger, great, thanks. MAROON OTTER still very relaxed*

and now over to the east side of Bradbury Road towards the junction with Princess Way.'

As I stayed in my position at a bus stop, I could see the cousins continuing to walk east away from the McDonalds and the office of MAROON OTTER. Absolutely no sign of White Team, which was great. I knew they would have control, but if we couldn't see them then the targets wouldn't be able to either.

'Base from Nine Four, that's MAROON OTTER back towards the entrance of the office, all yours.'

'Base have seen, that's MAROON OTTER now IN IN to the work address.'

'Team Leader, roger that, we are back towards you now. HARBOUR FISH has gone to his home address, so we're leaving him there.'

'Base, roger that. For information, we'd like you to stay on MAROON OTTER for another hour then withdraw.'

As the team leader acknowledged the news from the operations officer at base, I knew I wouldn't get home again tonight. Fuck me, my wife would be struggling. That hour dragged as I moved into a position from which I could retrieve my vehicle from the car park.

As the team leader called for us to withdraw from the area, Base sent us hotel details to our phones. We didn't bother going back to Thames House for debrief because we'd be back on the ground in a few hours anyway. I'd checked into the hotel when I thought 'fuck it' and got back in the car.

It was getting late when I pulled up outside home, still with all my operational kit on. I knew Lucy had probably just fed our son and put him down.

Creeping through the front door and upstairs, I listened at the bedroom door for signs of life. The gentle breathing of them both told me they were asleep. Not wanting to risk waking the baby, I quietly but quickly whipped around the downstairs of the house. Bin bags were put at the front door ready to take outside when I left. I folded the clothes that Lucy had dried earlier that day and stacked fresh nappies next to the changing mat. Toys put away, bottles into the sterilizer ready for the morning. Pots back in the cupboard and cutlery back into the drawers. I swept the kitchen floor and wrote a quick note to Lucy before grabbing the bin bags and leaving the house.

Sorry, job is overrunning, tried to do as much as I could without waking you both. Be back in the morning hopefully. Love ya.

As I drove back to the hotel I asked myself, was I so detached from reality that I couldn't recognize I was spreading myself too thin or was my MI5 surveillance mindset completely taking over my personal life? My first response was, *Shut up Tom, stop being such a dick and get back to your team.*

I joined the military to belong to a family. An environment I never had as a kid. When I was recruited into MI5 I joined an even tighter family unit, my team. But now, with a real family of my own, I felt my loyalty being tested and I couldn't honestly decide how to deal with it. My family, or the country's freedom, I had no fucking idea which was more important.

6

HIDING IN PLAIN SIGHT

'Zero Six is in the area.'

It was dark, but thankfully the food and coffee I'd grabbed on the way down was kicking in, so I felt ready for tonight's job.

It was quite simple really. With MAROON OTTER's office being closed during the night it should be fairly easy for one of our tech teams to gain entry and plant eavesdropping devices, thus making sure we completely understood the full intelligence picture around the businessman.

'All stations, MAROON OTTER is showing up in the area of Willesden, to the east, on the junction of Wilkins Lane and Stockford Avenue.'

'Team Leader, roger. Stations, let's get control of MAROON OTTER quickly to allow the tech team to get on site.'

It only took a few minutes for us to get into the area. The target could be in a house, in a car, walking on the street or in a bar but we knew he was here somewhere. It was now a matter of pride who would be first to find him within the team.

We had cars, vans, motorbikes and people out on foot hunting for him.

'Zero Six is checking the bars on the east side of Wilkins Lane.'

The rest of the team were constantly updating the areas they had checked, along with compass directions. Walking into the first pub, I saw it was fairly busy but open enough for me to check for MAROON OTTER.

When people walk into a bar they do one of three things. Find the toilets, look for the friends they are meeting or go to the bar and order a drink. I needed to check the toilets and see if I could identify a staff exit out the back just in case. Walking through the pub, I scanned the area in front of me and off to my sides, keeping it nice and relaxed. If anyone in here was providing counter-surveillance the first thing they would look for was new faces entering.

Nothing so far. I could hear the rest of the team still searching. Into the men's and still nothing apart from a properly pissed guy swaying next to the urinal, struggling to undo the buttons on his jeans. I took the opportunity to quickly empty my bladder then headed back out towards the bar, which gave me a better opportunity to scan the floor for MAROON OTTER.

'Bottle of Bud,' I told the barman.

Anything served in green or brown glass is perfect for hiding how much you're actually drinking. If the target wasn't in here I'd have to neck the beer and leave; if he was I could be here for hours.

Taking up a natural position right at the end of the bar, I sat on a stool and paid for my bottle. The internal CCTV screen was just in front of me and there were enough people in the pub to mean no one was paying me any attention.

Nothing to my immediate left, nothing at the bar, keep scanning. Just as I went to take a big long swig of my drink, ready to leave, I caught sight of a group of people on the CCTV screen. Lowering my head as I lifted the bottle to my mouth, I gave a low, very quick, 'STAND BY STAND BY.'

It was enough to tell the team someone had control of MAROON OTTER. Hopefully one of them would recognize it was me.

'*Zero Six, do you have control of MAROON OTTER?*' Graeme, the team leader, was on it straight away. I replied to him with our covert messaging system, and knew I had to give the team more information.

Pulling my phone out of my pocket, I faked a phone call, using the people at the bar to hide my profile from MAROON OTTER while I was sending a transmission over the radio to my team. Normally our messages on the net are extremely short and fast because there is so much going on and so many people trying to get on the radio at the same time. Right now, I needed a bit more freedom.

'Where are you?' I paused with a smile and a nod. 'I'm at the pub on the corner, next to the supermarket. Come down for a few?' Pausing as if waiting for a reply. 'All right, cool, well if you finish mending that MAROON OTTER and do decide to come down I'm at the bottom end of the bar. Bring everyone down. It's pretty packed near the door though.' Slightly longer pause. 'All right, mate, might catch you all in a bit. Bye, mate, bye.'

The second my transmission ended I could hear the team responding.

'Team Leader roger the last. Base acknowledge MAROON OTTER is under control in the pub on the corner of Wilkins Lane and Cottle Road. Stations can I have three into the pub, two of which need to be a couple, someone direct on the front door of the pub and the rest of the team close in to support.'

Ordering another bottle, I got comfortable, slumping forward on my bar stool with the perfect view of MAROON OTTER. He'd picked a table slightly behind the door, which gave him a perfect view of everyone coming or going. It took all of sixty seconds before Karen and Emma walked in together and took a position at a high table, laughing and joking, the perfect cover. They were two women dressed nicely, drinking wine and having a good catch up. While Karen had her back to MAROON OTTER, Emma could see his position and everything he did, including moving towards the door or using his phone. Emma would give Karen any information she gleaned and, to prevent MAROON OTTER seeing anything suspicious, Karen would transmit for her. Crucially Emma could also help identify any of the five people he was sitting with.

Mark walked in a few minutes later, in full orange hi-vis workwear. It was another perfect cover, brash and loud – who'd wear that if they were trying not to be spotted, right? He went straight to the bar on the end closest to MAROON OTTER and the door. I could just about hear Mark asking what food they sold. As the conversation went on between the barman and Mark, he gave the cover story that he couldn't drink because he was waiting for his gaffer to pick him up and head to their site. Mark spent the next hour drinking coke, eating crisps and playing the bandit. He was close in to MAROON OTTER and could hear the conversation at his table.

We were in a busy pub, we could see and hear everything this guy was doing and yet it would be incredibly difficult for anyone to detect a surveillance operator in here, never mind four of us.

'From Base, just for information. Tech teams are towards the office soon. The entry team leader has told me that once they get in they only need sixty seconds and they'll be back out and clear of the area.'

'Team Leader, roger that. Eight Six, any other targets with MAROON OTTER?'

'Negative. He's relaxed at the table but has finished his drink.'

'Stations from Base, entry team is towards the office now.'

Understanding when a situation is likely to change is crucial. I noticed it on the screen in front of me just as Karen put it out on the radio: 'Stations, MAROON OTTER is sat up right on the edge of his chair. The rest of the people around his table are now standing.'

'Base roger.'

The team outside would be ready to take him on as he left.

Those of us inside the pub would have to stay and leave sporadically so we kept blending in. MAROON OTTER was getting up. Here we go.

'*MAROON OTTER is now standing, coat on,*' Karen said. '*He's tapping his pockets and has just pulled out some keys before putting them back in his pocket.*'

'*Tech Team, roger.*' Their team leader was listening in on our channel, and her whispered reply told us they were either gaining entry or already on target. Hopefully they would be out of the way soon.

'*Stations inside the pub, from Charlie Six One, two taxis have just pulled up outside.*'

'*Team Leader, roger that.*'

I could see the group of friends and MAROON OTTER moving towards the door on the screen in front of me as Karen gave the covert signal on her radio that he was leaving the pub. It's the same signal we use for a stand by when we see a target, designed to wake everyone up on the net to something very important happening right now.

'*Charlie Six One has control of MAROON OTTER leaving the pub and straight into the back of the first taxi. A black Addison Lee Ford Galaxy. VRN, Tango Echo six six Victor Victor Yankee.*'

'*Team Leader, roger, we'll go with this.*'

'*Base roger, Tech Team are on site.*'

Taking a drink of my beer, I didn't physically react to the team outside, but I did start to wonder if MAROON

OTTER was going home or back to the office for something.

'*That's the taxi now westbound on the Alpha four zero seven, passing the red double decker on his near side.*'

'*Tech Team, roger. Can you give us a countdown if it continues towards us? We can extract in ten seconds.*'

'*Roger that, Tech Team, will do. And from Charlie Six One that's the vehicle still westbound and now showing a left-hand indication. For information this will keep him on the Alpha four zero seven generally towards the office.*'

'*Base, roger, MAROON OTTER also has a girlfriend on Cornish Park just south of the office address.*'

The team comms were nearly constant between the control car, base and the tech team, who were still inside the office. Karen, Emma, Mark and me were still in the pub with the rest of the punters. We'd leave in stages, Mark being the first to go, given his cover story.

As the team followed the taxi ever closer to the area of the office, the tech team popped up on the net. '*Tech Team Leader, permission?*'

'*Go ahead, taxi is now showing a right-hand indication at the junction of Cornish Park.*'

'*Roger, Tech Team has extracted to the north and install successful.*'

'*Base, roger. Green Team cease and withdraw, I'll notify the other teams to do the same.*'

'*Green Team, roger. All stations, can we start the phased*

extraction of the guys inside the pub please, starting with Charlie Two Seven to collect your builder!'

As Mark gave the tones to acknowledge he was the one to be picked up first, I ordered another beer. I could see Karen and Emma had nearly finished their glasses of wine and, while still busy, the pub was starting to swing towards a more male bias. The later we stayed the more they'd stand out.

It took around ten minutes for Mark to leave. I could see the white van that pulled up outside to pick him up. With orange lights on the top and magnetic signage on the sides, it looked every inch a work van. Emma and Karen got the clear signal to leave the pub, and one of our team picked them up around the corner. Now just me.

'Zero Six, when you feel ready to leave, walk south towards Cottle Road and then go right and east on Cottle Road towards the station. I'll pick you up there. Stations, happy for everyone else to get back to the garages for debrief. Team Leader out.'

Finishing my beer, I used the toilet and walked casually out. I tried to gauge any reaction to me, as I had done when the others had left. Nothing. All good, nice and easy.

The cool night air hit my face straight away as I took the two turns towards the tube station. It's at times like this we have to be careful not to get a false sense of security. There was a kid on a scooter swerving round and a few passing cars but nothing to be overly worried about.

I could see Graeme's car up in the distance waiting for me, parked so that I could climb in without crossing the road or walking round the vehicle. Suddenly I couldn't wait to get home. I almost wanted to run so we could get the debrief done and I could see my family for that little bit of extra time.

I walked towards the passenger side of Graeme's car. The engine wasn't on and his profile was hidden pretty well. I had my hand on the door handle when I heard engine revs. Then I saw a scooter with two blokes on the back, all in black, including their helmets.

Fuck, protect Graeme! Autopilot took over. Sprinting around the back of the car, I saw the guys were already at Graeme's door, smashing the window with a crowbar, the guy on the back doing the work, the rider screaming the instructions.

'Gear! Gis' the gear NOW!'

Graeme switched his engine on, as we're well drilled to do when something like this happens. As I came behind the scooter I could see the crowbar about to come down on Graeme, now that his window had completely gone.

No fucking way are you doing this to my team leader, no fucking way!

When you've got a helmet on it makes you vulnerable to attack, limits your vision. I had to exploit this to let Graeme get away.

Just as the crowbar was coming down I lurched forwards, wrapping my fingers underneath the sides of the passenger's helmet into the sponge fabric inside. I pulled backwards and to the side, away from Graeme's car.

'Go GO!' I shouted to him.

He didn't but the scooter screamed off with a high-pitched buzz while the passenger scrambled up from the ground.

Obviously not ready for a fight, he turned to run and I started to follow, the blood burning as it rocketed around my veins.

The bear hug stopped me instantly, along with a quiet but firm whisper in my ear: 'Tom, enough. Let's go!'

I got into the passenger side of the car and Graeme drove us out of there, bursting a few red traffic lights as he radioed in a description of the attackers.

'Base, roger the last, I'll let the other teams and Special Branch know. All stations, security checks every sixty seconds please.'

Graeme drove around, taking an obscure route to get back to my car, but other than talking on the radio, he didn't say anything. Maybe he was suffering a bit of shock. When he pulled up around the corner from my car, he looked at me.

'Are you OK?' he asked.

'Yeah fine, I didn't get hit. Are you? Did that crowbar connect?'

He was still covered in bits of glass from the window and the fabric of his top had obviously been grabbed and pawed at around the arms.

'Tom, I can understand why you went for them but you weren't going to stop, were you?'

Holy shit, this was a dressing down. This was so confusing. 'I was protecting you!'

'I get that and you did,' Graeme said calmly. 'It was quick thinking, but once the scooter fucked off and that guy was ready to run we had enough room to get out of there. You should have jumped straight into the car and we could have driven away.'

I sat silently while Graeme gave a quick security check, followed by the rest of the team. Rubbing the back of my hand on my sore bottom lip, I saw a thin layer of blood. I'd bitten into my lip when I took that guy on. Graeme noticed it.

'You weren't in control there, mate. Your aggression took over. Biting your lip in a fight is a clear sign, you know that!'

'What we gonna do?' I wasn't pleading for Graeme not to grass me up. It was his team, he was the team leader and had got there by merit. I trusted him. I just wanted to know what was coming. The worst thing that could happen to any member of the team was to be taken off the road while there was an investigation, maybe stuck in a support admin job like making sure the team's cars were serviced.

A smile crept over Graeme's mouth but his voice was still fairly stern. 'I'll handle it.'

Nodding thankfully, I opened the door to go back to my car just as he hit me with something else. 'Mate, if you need to talk, make sure you do.'

I didn't. No desire to talk at all. I made it into my car just in time for the next round of security checks which was shorter now, as some of the team were back in the garages. *Talk?* What would I need to talk about? I'm fucking MI5. The only thing I want to talk about is getting home quicker!

Driving through the streets, making up as much ground as possible, my mind kept switching from Graeme to my wife and family. He was right, I had been out of control. We have continuous training for this sort of stuff from guys in the military. One of the instructors, a man I'd known for years, would tell me, 'Tom, remember on the day of the race you need to breathe. You could be fighting for a long time until help arrives. Most fights are over in seconds, make sure you can last beyond that. Breathe and control your aggression.'

I would always be the 'demo man', the person used to demonstrate strikes, holds or counter strikes in close-quarters situations. Unfortunately, I had a habit of treating training as real-world events; my control of a situation would slip and I'd resort to full violence, which would be thought of as a step too far.

Yep, Graeme was right; I had lost control and put myself in harm's way without thinking. I could feel the cloud of disappointment slowly casting a shadow over me. The tears in my eyes were starting to hinder my driving. I was almost back at the garages and needed to sort myself out, not let the team see me like this. I didn't want anyone to think I was weak or out of control. I wanted them to know they could rely on me, like my family.

But now, feeling like I'd fucked up, I realized I relied on them and my wife more than they'd ever know.

The next day a different team was rotated in to take over the surveillance, to avoid any chance of compromise. The cousins were eventually arrested before they could commit an act of terrorism and thanks to the eavesdropping devices in his office, any threat from MAROON OTTER was neutralized.

7

FIND, STOP, REPEAT

Some operations can last for months, some targets can stay on our radar for years. And some days you are scrambling with only hours to stop an atrocity from a clean skin. You never know what is coming, and you need to be mentally prepared to handle whatever the situation throws at you.

A few years after Operation STARLING, the pace of operations, never slow to start with, had picked up.

My phone had been vibrating for less than a second when I reached down the side of the bed to read the message:

FULL TEAM ON AIR 10 MINUTES.

Fuck. I knew this would be messing with Lucy's plans for us.

Even though I was meant to be at home that day, and watching my son's nursery nativity play in the afternoon, the night before I'd still put my operational kit and clothes next to my side of the bed, along with a fully charged phone. Sliding out of the bed without any fuss, I got dressed and was out of the door and into my team car three minutes later. The digital clock on my old Ford Escort was reading 04.36. It was pitch black as I waited to start the engine. I let the handbrake off and the gentle slope of the hill slowly took control of the car. When we leave or arrive at home, we do it with minimal fuss. The last thing you want is to make the area your family live in red hot by spinning your wheels and showing out.

I turned the ignition with the clutch dipped and the car sprang to life. I got on the radio. 'Charlie Nine Six Eight is on air.'

'Roger that from Team Leader. Good morning. Just waiting for the rest of the team and we'll get a briefing from Ops, but for now head towards Liverpool please.'

'Charlie Nine Six Eight, roger.'

Heading towards the motorway, I passed a set of traffic lights with two cars side by side at a roundabout. A Honda Civic full of young lads hanging out of the window looking at the car next to it, a brand-new Mercedes S-Class in black. It was immaculate. Like the paint was still wet. A great-looking car. As they both left the roundabout and took off at speed in a different direction to me, I thought about the car I was in; Charlie Nine Six Eight.

All our team vehicles serve a purpose. Whether technically or operationally, everything we do has a purpose. So today I was in my ripped tracksuit bottoms and dirty sweatshirt, driving a dirty, old, dull-blue Ford Escort. Why? Because in the areas we usually work in, no one is looking twice at someone like me in a car like this.

The job is never about jumping over bonnets wearing

aviators. It's always about getting the maximum amount of intelligence without being seen, in order to keep people alive.

It didn't take long before everyone had confirmed they were on the air.

'*Good morning Green Team,*' Base said. '*Apologies for the early call out. I know most of you haven't had much time at home. This is a first look with a view to get immediate Executive Action on a brand-new target that came in last night for Operation ANT-EATER. One station so far . . .*'

It's always good practice when briefing over the air to give breaks and check the team are still receiving all the information without signal drop-outs.

'*Team Leader, so far.*'

'*The target is SPACE JUNK, details and images have been uploaded to your PDAs. We don't have a specific location for him yet. You need to find him. Once you do we'll bring in the Executive Action team that's on stand by, ready for you.*'

Jobs like this are normally quick and clean.

'*Overnight intelligence is showing that SPACE JUNK intends to firebomb a local school. Last known location was in the area of the university and Edge Hill to the east. We'll update you as more comes in. Base out.*'

'*Team Leader, roger. Everyone to the last known area and we'll split the team, half on foot, half in vehicles.*'

Switching my PDA on, I searched through the target list until I found SPACE JUNK's file. I could see he was white, twenty-two years old, with a large scar down the right side of his face. There were no known vehicles attached to him, but that didn't mean he wouldn't be driving or be a passenger. With him being a brand-new target and this a first look, it just meant he hadn't got a driving licence, vehicles registered in his name or registered to the addresses he was associated with.

Once the initial flurry of transmissions were over, the radio went silent, like technical tumbleweed. I hated the quiet radio on long drives, feeling isolated from the team. It was a relief to reach the Liverpool area.

'*Bravo One Zero is in the area of Edge Hill now.*'

Emma, as most bikers normally are, was first into the area and searching. Today we had her as well as Ryan on this operation. This target was obviously being thought of as a terrorist, otherwise we wouldn't be getting involved. The intelligence officers would know all the details from all the different reports that constantly came across their desks. The information given to our team was thin, but to be honest it didn't matter. We didn't need to know the ins and outs of who SPACE JUNK was affiliated to or his ideology at this point. If it was a long-term operation then we would have detailed briefings but right here and now we had his picture. That was enough for us to hunt him down and prevent him trying to kill children.

It wasn't long before the rest of us slid into the area. Being December, it was still dark and would be for a while, but the place was starting to wake up with people travelling early to work. Soon the school runs would begin. The streets were soaking wet from the hard rain driving down.

'Charlie Nine Six Eight is in the area, checking the western part of Edge Hill.'

When we roll into a neighbourhood, especially one as tight as this, we need to search in a way that doesn't light the area up. No normal person clocks a vehicle or person on the street at first sight unless they are doing something out of the ordinary, but if you start doubling back, taking corners too quickly, engine revs too high or speed too slow it all raises your profile to the locals. It's the same when you're on foot checking, you can't be constantly swivelling left to right like a bobble head on speed.

Spotting the chance to cover a major junction, after first checking the side streets for anyone who vaguely looked like SPACE JUNK, I pulled over just short of a cafe that some local builders were already making good use of.

As I waited near the counter for my greasy sausage and egg cob and cheap coffee, I took the opportunity to glance at the five builders in there. None of them were the target. Watching the street through the window while listening to these guys debate football, I caught sight of one of our team cars driving past, still searching. They had spotted my car parked up.

'*Zero Six, have you got the junction of Grove Street and Lowe Hill?*'

I gave the reply for yes used in situations when we are unable to talk openly and got a quick reply. '*Roger the yes yes, I'll hold further north towards the hospital.*'

'*Team Leader, roger. All stations, we'll take up static positions now and wait for him to come to us or Base to offer something up. When it gets busier we'll start roaming again.'*

'Sausage and egg. Brown sauce?'

'Ta.'

Having already paid, and despite being in the North, I didn't offer anything else up in terms of a reply. It wasn't needed. Sitting at a table at the back of the cafe furthest away from the window, I watched the world go by outside, knowing that anyone walking past would spot the group of builders in front of me but would be unlikely to notice or even be able to see me without coming in.

Making use of the paper in front of me, I flicked through, taking my time with the food and coffee. Still nothing. Sometimes you don't need to even directly observe what's going on – just being in tune with the people around you can highlight when someone has walked in or the mood changes for the worse.

'Stations, quick update from Base. We don't have any associated known targets of SPACE JUNK and no technical assets in play.'

Fuck, where was he? I glanced out of the window again. A man was walking past in a black parka but he was too old to be our target.

'STAND BY STAND BY from Eight Six, I have control of SPACE JUNK walking west on Falkner Square near the park. Green jacket, black trousers, carrying a grey rucksack, which looks full.'

Karen had caught him. I'd already started to take my last

bite as soon as I heard the first stand by. Walking normally, I left the cafe and got into my car, driving away around the block then getting on the power to make sure Karen had the support she needed. The whole team were trying to get in on this.

'Base, roger. Executive Action is now five minutes out.'

As I closed in, listening to Karen's commentary on SPACE JUNK, I could see some of our team on foot ready to assist with the follow. Meanwhile, Base was giving countdowns on the arrival of the armed police team.

'From Eight Six, SPACE JUNK is now running towards the junction of Upper Duke Street, five zero metres short.'

'From Base, there are several schools in this immediate area, Executive Action is two minutes out.'

'Eight Six, you can let him run to the junction – I'm there now.'

'Roger. Thank you, Six Eight, all yours.'

Mark being ahead at the junction had prevented the need for Karen to start running after SPACE JUNK.

'Six Eight has control, SPACE JUNK still running towards Upper Duke Street, this is westbound. He's got one arm behind him trying to support his rucksack, which looks like it's wet at the bottom.'

'Base, roger, I'm relaying your comms now to the strike team, please keep it constant.'

'Six Eight, roger that. SPACE JUNK is across the junction now on the south side still running west on Upper Duke Street with the large trees of the park to his left.'

Mark's constant commentary was vital to the strike team

nailing the target quickly. I was in a position behind Karen, ready to pick her up if she needed it, when the first of the police vehicles came barrelling past, no lights or sirens, but extremely quick. Mark kept it coming.

'*SPACE JUNK is still westbound, trying to stop the rucksack from bouncing on his back, running on the south side, past the bus stop two zero metres from the junction of Rodney Street.*

'*Base, SPACE JUNK hasn't seen the first strike vehicle coming at him from the west, he's just run past the police undercover car parked up on the north side.*'

Obviously this guy was so focused on what he was about to do that he'd missed the two armed police officers in black kit in an unmarked BMW, and hadn't noticed the headlights screaming towards him.

'*Stations, from Six Eight, Executive Action team now out on foot taking control of target. Base, I will keep eyes on until he's definitely secure.*'

'*Roger, thanks, talking to their team commander now.*'

Two more vehicles, now with sirens and lights, came blasting past as I eased into a space in a row of parked cars just in front of Karen. She got into the car without any fuss and we went through the fake show of smiles and friendliness as I pulled out and took the first turning right, wanting to move out of sight. Normally the strike teams like to come in fast and leave with the target quickly but once they have control we never stick around, just in case the locals turn investigative journalists.

'*From Six Eight, SPACE JUNK is being plasti-cuffed on the*

floor, backpack removed. Team Leader, I'm lifting off this, they have control.'

'Job done.' I nodded to Karen, whose smile turned to a scowl when she noticed my dirty top.

'Is that brown sauce? You had breakfast, ya fucker?!'

I was laughing from the pit of my stomach as Karen directed me back to her car.

'All in the name of living my cover.'

'Bollocks, you fat bastard!'

Karen's banter was interrupted by an update from the base back in Thames House operations room: *'Green Team, cease and withdraw, happy to do the debrief on air to get you all home quicker. Is that OK, Team Leader?'*

'Yes yes, all stations acknowledge down the list and foot crews call up when you are complete with your vehicles again.'

The team responded to the cease and withdraw order from Base as I dropped Karen off at her car and drove out of the area on streets I hadn't used yet this morning. I saw Emma in my mirrors as I came to a stop at a set of red lights. I knew she'd spotted my car when she peeled off right, taking a different route to me to avoid moving in a convoy of surveillance vehicles. Even when the threat of a target is removed we still make sure we blend in. It doesn't stop. The operational awareness is engrained into us so much that it consumes our thought processes every waking minute, and most sleeping ones too.

'Green Team from Base, debrief commencing at 0906 hours on Operation ANTEATER. One station acknowledge?'

'Team Leader, roger.'

'*Thank you. SPACE JUNK is now in police custody. I've spoken with their command and the backpack he was carrying was full of petrol bombs. He's already started to talk about the intended target of non-white children and, I quote, "Fucking paki cunts and their rats, they should burn." I'll spare you the rest.*'

It's not very often we get terrorists who fall into the bracket of white supremacist, and racism falls under the remit of the police. But this guy wanted to kill children because they weren't white and by the sounds of it he wanted to do so to further his own ideology. We prevented that. Right now, these children were bouncing into school looking for their favourite friend, wondering what their parents had put in their lunchboxes, some so young they had only just started full days. They were blissfully unaware that a top-secret operation which had begun while they were asleep was brought to an end just metres from the school gates.

Once the debrief had ended, I had nothing to do except drive and think. The time to think is an operator's worst enemy. We deal with the world's shit so no one else has to see it. Somehow we need to find a way to process it and move on, but for me that was easier said than done. As usual my mind was dwelling on all the what ifs. What if we hadn't found SPACE JUNK? What if he got away from us? How much damage would he have done? It strikes much harder when kids are in danger. During the operation itself the team will be as clinical and focused as always, but dealing with the after effects is tough.

I was held at a set of red lights on a major junction about an hour from home and my son's nursery school, thinking that hopefully I'd be in time to meet Lucy there and watch his first nativity.

The sky suddenly gets darker. A storm must be on the way and I'm probably right under a massive raincloud. The driver of the car in front is getting impatient, head turning from one set of lights to the other, both stuck on red for what feels like forever.

Light flashes across my view straight into the car in front, from the driver's side to the passenger side. *What the . . . ?* More flashes. Then the noise. *FUCK.* The sound of gunfire is unmistakable, deafening. The driver is down as the rounds continue to rip into the car on full auto. No sign of the gunman yet.

'SHOTS FIRED SHOTS FIRED, ZERO SIX!' Fuck, the radios are down.

The car in front starts to catch fire.

There's a truck directly behind me, no chance of reversing out of there. As the flames lick their way around the outside of the car, faster and higher, I feel pure fear. *Get out, get out now!* Pulling at the door handle, I realize it's broken. If I don't do something I'll die here. I've got to assume they are coming for me. Headlights on full beam from the truck fill my mirrors as a motorbike coming from the right slams into the car in front, sending the rider right over the top to be instantly hit by an oncoming vehicle.

The bike is embedded in the car, surrounded by flames.

Screams from pedestrians drown everything out apart from the constant sound of a car horn.

Either I'm about to get hit or someone else is going to be killed; I can't let either happen. I pull at my seat belt but it's stuck. The flashing headlights, the constant horn, fire, screams, they are all blending into one. I can't get out. The headlights are so bright they are overpowering the darkness created by the clouds. Too bright, too loud, the light and noise burning into my head, searing pain like a nail being driven into my temple. In that split second I question whether I've been hit by the gunman I haven't identified yet. Is that what the pain is?

Knock knock knock on the window. 'Excuse me, you OK?'

'AARRGGGHHHHH!' I screamed at the overweight pensioner using his walking stick to tap on my driver's side window. He recoiled back in his mobility scooter. What the fuck was he thinking? He should be finding somewhere to hide.

Another beep and flash of the headlights from the truck behind me. I turned my head and saw it lurch forward towards my car, trying to push me on. I tried my seat belt again and it popped straight away. *Make your move now.* I prayed the door handle would work this time, otherwise I'd be going out of the window. It did. Flying out of the car, I hit the pavement, looking for the threat. People were everywhere. Spinning around, I thought, *If I can make myself the focus of fire it could help save the people around me.*

No one is running. Why are they still here? Wait. Why are they looking at me?

I tried to get my bearings while shooting pains sparked across my head, leaving little trails of light in my vision. I could see the truck manoeuvring around my car as the driver leaned out of his window. 'You fucking wanker,' he shouted, giving me the hand gesture to back up his statement.

The people on the street were walking past me as a long line of traffic moved past my car. There was no burning vehicle, no crashed motorbike, no gunman. Nothing.

There was only normality there. My heart rate was through the roof and I felt sick and dizzy.

Getting back in my car just as the traffic lights flicked to green, I drove away from the carnage that never was. *Control your breathing. Slow it down.* I wasn't sure what was happening, except I had imagined everything I'd just seen. *Bury it. It didn't happen.*

I used the next hour or so to try and reassure myself that I was OK. I knew where I was and what had just happened was a daydream of sorts. I arrived at my son's school just in time. Running in, I looked like a scruffy dad, still in my operational kit and clothes, but it didn't really matter, Lucy would be happy I was there. Her eyes lit up as I walked into the small school hall, which was already filled with waiting parents. She had saved me a seat, just in case.

'You made it!'

The smile on Lucy's face instantly put me at peace.

As nativity plays go, it was fairly standard. Teachers were

sitting at the side of a small makeshift stage with the lines, ready to help the little ones out when they forgot and corral any toddlers who tried to make a run for it. My son was a shepherd, wearing a costume made from a sheet, with a tea-towel on his head. Whenever he looked our way Lucy and I would wave and give him a thumbs up. He was growing up fast and despite me wanting to devote every waking second I had to my family, I felt I had no choice but to be with the team as well. What we did today and always do is important. We keep people alive.

I was watching my son's face as he absorbed the other children around him when a small window behind us slammed shut, making a few of the parents jump. I was one of them. Lucy looked instantly quizzical. I don't jump. Normally. Reaching for my hand, she squeezed it to offer reassurance. Instinctively, she must have known I wasn't in balance. Although I never talked to her about what was happening on the job, the fact she had been in Special Operations in Northern Ireland meant she had a broad sense of what my work entailed.

Fuck. My eyes welled up just as the nativity came to an end. *Swallow it Tom, don't let this control you. You're OK.*

I wasn't. I couldn't let my family see something was wrong, that I wasn't coping with the things I was seeing.

There were tears streaming down my face as all the parents stood up and headed towards the stage.

'I'm *so* proud of you, you were the best shepherd I've ever seen!' Giving my son a big cuddle, I lifted him up to look at his smiling face. His hand rubbed my cheek.

'Daddy, your face is wet.'

Forcing the biggest smile I could muster, I passed him to Lucy. One of the other parents rubbed my shoulder.

'It gets me every time too,' she said.

'He's always like this, a big softy!' Lucy replied as I used my sleeves to wipe the tears from my face. The fake smile was fixed firmly until I'd regained control.

Lucy knew. She knew I wasn't in control. I was in freefall. Why couldn't I be normal?

I didn't tell anyone about the strange flashback and I put it out of my mind. True, I'd been having the occasional nightmare in the years since leaving Northern Ireland, but I could ignore that too. Keeping busy was the answer.

Everybody's hiding something, even if it's only from themselves.

8

THE BEST SPIES IN THE WORLD

Most people think of MI5 as stopping terrorists from killing hundreds of people and while that's true, there is another side of our job – to make sure our way of life actually survives. Imagine how different your day would be without the ability to take cash out, without the internet powering everything, from information systems right through to control signals for our railways. Without fucking electricity or running water. While we are the best in the world at keeping people safe from maniac suicide bombers, there are much bigger threats to this country in the form of cyberwarfare and state-sponsored espionage from states like China and Russia. The stakes were always raised when Russia was involved, and it felt as if everyone in the team sat a little straighter in their seats in the A4 briefing room at Thames House when the operations officer, Alison, said, 'Your target is MAGENTA STOAT, part of Operation GIGANTIC.'

Probably one of our highest-priority targets of the past few years. Not just in terms of the Russians, but overall.

MAGENTA STOAT was, for the desk officer, an intelligence goldmine, but one that hardly ever came out into the open. He'd only ever been seen once by our surveillance operators doing anything operational.

'MAGENTA STOAT is expected to be meeting a contact at some point today. He's a big Chelsea fan, and we have intelligence to indicate he will be going to today's match at Stamford Bridge.'

Football games and the crowds that they bring are the ultimate double-edged sword for operators like us. While being able to hide among thousands of people is a gift, it also makes it difficult to keep a visual on the targets. Sometimes we would have to be within touching distance just to be able to see them.

'Obviously we need to keep control of him throughout the day. He's got a box for the game so he won't be in the main stands. It would make sense for him to have some sort of meet inside the stadium given the level of security there. However, as you all know, the Russians are the *second* best in the world at this . . .'

A few laughs rippled through the team.

'Team Leader, we need as much video and audio as possible on MAGENTA STOAT,' Alison went on. 'We cannot risk a compromise. I would rather lose control of the target and any possible contacts than alert him to surveillance.'

This was a serious point, we all knew it. Sometimes we pushed the envelope of what's tactical and secure in order to get the best intelligence. The fact we were being told the desk would rather have a loss than a compromise only highlighted how sensitive this target was.

When we get a target it's because they are a threat to life and/or a risk to our national security. We go after the targets that are the highest risks and sometimes the most sensitive. MAGENTA STOAT was definitely the latter.

Pete, in front of me, raised his arm to ask Alison a question.

'What's MAGENTA STOAT's end game?'

Pete wasn't new to A4, he'd been with the teams for years, but he'd never worked on a high-profile Russian before. Sometimes it just falls that way. However, it was a question Alison wasn't going to answer.

'With respect, Pete, it's need to know and I need you guys to be completely impartial on the ground. The circle of intelligence is limited to me, Director A and the DG, as well as one or two in Vauxhall.'

Director A was the head of A Branch, the DG was the Director General of MI5. There was a very tense silence in the room, a mixture of Pete asking the wrong question and Alison taking our curiosity out of the loop.

Alison broke the silence as she continued, 'What I can tell you is that MAGENTA STOAT is our number-one priority right now. The intelligence that he is meeting a contact is extremely reliable, but we don't know when or where. That's what you are going to find out today. Once you have identified the contact, they need housing. Russians being Russians, we need to keep control of MAGENTA STOAT too.'

Someone getting ranked so highly is not to be taken lightly. My gut was telling me that MAGENTA STOAT didn't just pose a threat to national security but was highly likely to be a very credible threat to our nation as a whole.

As Alison walked out of the briefing room, we started to discuss tactics, where we would pick MAGENTA STOAT up from and, if a contact was identified, how we would keep hold of them both. Splitting a team up isn't ideal for a number of reasons, mainly because it exposes you. With more operators on the ground you can rotate around the target constantly, but the fewer people you have to do that the harder it becomes to stay invisible. Our team leader had one priority though: to make sure every single member of our team came home.

As we all headed down to the cars in the garage, the team leader shouted the channel we were going to be using on the radios today: 'Channel three please, guys.'

The profile break-up of our team was, as always, massively diverse, with a 50/50 split between male and female, ages ranging from young to old, and a mix of ethnicities. Not one of us would wear the same branded clothing, unlike other surveillance units outside MI5 who would mostly be wearing Merrell walking shoes, a North Face or Rab jacket and blue jeans. We don't do that. Ever. There should be nothing that allows a third party to connect the members of our team.

Throwing my kit and camera bags into the boot of my beaten up Mazda 6, I looked across to Sarah, who was unlocking a brand-new Mercedes E-Class and putting her kit in the boot.

'What the fuck? Why am I driving this piece of shit and you get that?!' I joked.

Sarah, who was dressed in heels and a smart suit finished off with a shawl, replied confidently, 'We need to split the profile of the team up. You go into shit areas, I'll take him on if he goes back into Kensington.'

Laughing, I got into my car, switching the radio onto channel three. 'Anyone read Charlie Eight Nine for a comms check?'

I might be a bit eager here, since no one was on just yet. I'd need to wait a few seconds for a response before driving out though. There's no point getting on the ground if your radio isn't working.

'Anyone read Charlie Eight Nine for a comms check please?'

'*Yeah, loud and clear to Charlie Seven Seven.*' Sarah had just switched onto channel three.

'Roger, thanks mate, likewise.'

Andy popped up straight away on the net. '*Does your chauffeur know the way, Charlie Seven Seven?*'

Looking up, I could see the rest of the team beaming and laughing in their cars. Brilliant. This type of camaraderie allowed our team to stay tight-knit, strong and focused.

Making my way out of the garage, following behind our biker Mark, I drove towards the area of Stamford Bridge, waiting to get the game plan and our start point from the team leader. This was potentially going to be a very long day and we were going up against the very best Russia had to offer.

'From Team Leader, all stations, can you head to the area of Stamford Bridge, specifically the hotel at the south-east corner. First into that area can you shout up please.'

As the team acknowledged, I flicked through the maps to the page with Stamford Bridge, Chelsea's football stadium. I was thinking about the profiles of our team, who would be suitable to go inside, who had what technical kit. The team leader had obviously been given a heads-up from the operations officer back in Thames House that the hotel was a good starting point, but the lack of detailed information coming through was clearly directly linked to MAGENTA STOAT being such a high priority target. It was another reminder that he was not only a threat to us as a nation, but that this was an incredibly sensitive situation.

It didn't take me long to navigate through the London traffic, but Mark was first in the area. Unless you wear your pants on the outside of your trousers and your last name is Kent, you aren't going to be faster than one of our bikers across big cities.

'That's Bravo Nine in the area now. Place is rammed.'

'Roger that, Bravo Nine, any other stations close by?'

'Yeah, Charlie Eight Eight is two minutes out to the east.'

'Roger that, Charlie Eight Eight. Can you ditch your car? I need you on foot today. Stations, just be aware we have assets in place inside the stadium. We will take on any and all contacts. We have Red and Blue teams on stand by to help if we need them.'

Fucking hell, this was a big job. It's not that often we have another team ready to come and help us out – it happens only when there are a lot of targets in play – but this would be the very first time I'd ever seen two entire teams on stand by to give support. It felt as if the stakes were being ramped up with each transmission.

I was going to be on foot all day, which meant I would have to try and blend in with the football crowds right now and potentially be able to blend into another part of London later.

Parking my car down a side street, I decided to walk the rest of the way. Just as I got out of the car and flicked my hood up over my baseball cap, joining a large group of Chelsea supporters, my radio kicked in with a message. I could hear the engine of the motorbike dropping down the gears before Mark started talking.

'*Team Leader or Base, have we got agent handlers in play on this job?*'

Silence. The sort of technical tumbleweed that every operator hates but tells you everything you need to know. Having agent handlers on the ground happens all the time but normally it plays out in one of two ways. We know when they are likely to cross into our operation or if they are working close to the targets we are watching, *or* we let the agent handler know when we are out of the area and they can go about their business.

Still nothing. I decided to prompt a response quietly while within the crowd. 'You are going out mate, loud and clear.'

'*Bravo Nine, roger, thanks Zero Six.*'

Still no response from the team leader or the operations officer back at Thames. We never ignore transmissions from people within the team – that could potentially be fatal either for us on the ground or the wider public. I took the silence to mean that the team leader was talking to Base about the agent handler being in the area. Whatever the reason for the lack of response, Mark was our teammate, so everyone took the initiative, starting with Sarah.

'Charlie Seven Seven is local to you, Bravo Nine. To the west, covering Fulham Road.'

'Bravo Nine, you have One Six to the north towards the cemetery.'

The positions kept piling in from everyone else in the team, like a set of Spartan soldiers working in complete unison.

'Stations, quick update from Team Leader. There are other assets in play. Obviously if MAGENTA STOAT meets a friendly asset we don't need to take them on.'

Welcome to MI5! Quite often operators are given relevant intelligence, but only enough to ensure we have the upper hand while still staying impartial about what we are seeing. If we are told a target is going to do something specific that day we will look for evidence to fit that picture. But there are a lot of different components to intelligence work. Surveillance is a very crucial part of this jigsaw but we can only report on what we can see – not what we assume is happening. It's the desk officers back in Thames House who fit eight billion pieces together and come up with an incredibly accurate intelligence picture of what a target's intentions are.

The team leader's last transmission was clear: we weren't going to be told about any potential parallel operations today. We would discuss the ins and outs of it all when we finished this job, but right now we needed to concentrate and be a team. The Thames House geeks run that show, out here we control the ground.

'*Zero Six from Bravo Nine, are you close to the stadium? I need to move off.*'

I could hear the chanting over Mark's transmission. The crowds and no doubt heavy police presence would eventually clock a motorbike hanging around.

'Yes mate, I can see the stadium now,' I said, picking up my pace subtly. 'I'm just coming over the bridge to the east.'

'*Roger, thanks. Team Leader, Bravo Nine will hold out further west and wait for a stand by.*'

'*Roger that, thank you. Stations, I want several more out on foot to support Zero Six and One Six. All compass directions, focus attention on the cemetery to the north of the stadium and I need two vehicles further south-west in the area of the park – Eel Brook Common.*'

The team again responded quickly to the team leader's request, listening to each other's positions.

The crowds were massive, thousands of people everywhere. The chanting and football banter was mostly good-natured but I could feel an undertone of aggression building. I wasn't worried though – there was a heavy police presence with riot vans, uniforms on foot, horses, the whole gamut of public order policing as well as a strategically placed camera van looking for known offenders.

It was now a waiting game as the entire team started blending into the area, becoming part of the crowd. Joining a small group of people in a queue at a burger van, I tuned into my environment more, seeing the odd family mixed in with pockets of supporters wearing team shirts and scarves. The burger was overpriced but it could be a long time before I got another chance to eat.

'*Stations from Base, MAGENTA STOAT is confirmed inside Stamford Bridge. MAGENTA STOAT INSIDE the stadium. Team Leader, I should be able to get confirmation to you once he is leaving. He's not expected to stay to watch the game. Base out.*'

'*Team Leader, roger that. Stations, with that in mind can we have eyes on every possible exit please.*'

A quick look at my watch told me there was still an hour till kick off. From my position I could see one of the main entrances, the Shed End, just past the hotel in front of me. I had to be careful because if I stayed in one spot rather than moving into the stadium I might draw the attention of police on the lookout for organized crime – ticket touts, that sort of thing.

Hiding my speech with my burger, I updated the team leader. 'Zero Six has the Shed End to the south-east corner.'

With nothing to do but watch and wait I started to think about the targets MAGENTA STOAT was ranked above.

I was sure this went way beyond the usual problems caused by hostile foreign intelligence. *Bollocks, no time to think about that now.* Just as I leaned against a wall to keep an eye on the stadium exit, two large crowds of Chelsea and away team fans started to exchange abuse. It immediately caught the eye of the police and they began to circle in a well-drilled motion.

'Guys from Zero Six, there is trouble with the fans at the Shed End south-east corner, avoid it if you can.'

I had a choice here: leave and risk missing MAGENTA STOAT coming out or take my chances and hope the police got control fast.

'Team Leader, roger that, Zero Six. We don't have any other way of keeping eyes on that exit yet.'

I had to stay in position. I could move around a bit but the police were swarming in fast, horses shouldering their way forward, towering over the supporters, followed by well over twenty uniformed officers trying to identify and deal with the main instigators from both groups. One of the horses rotated around and I found myself a few feet away from its hind legs. *Shit, if this horse kicks out and hits me I'm a dead man.* Moving away, I followed the wall around, walking calmly but not slowly enough to look sinister. The police would be twitchy, watching for that one renegade who acts as a catalyst.

The volume of the shouting from both the police and the group of now nearly one hundred people was so loud it drowned out the transmission that had just been sent over the radio. *Fuck.* I couldn't keep this position secure anymore. If I couldn't hear messages being sent by base or anyone else on the ground, I was not an effective part of the team. I took cover where two brick walls met in the hope I could make out exactly what was being said over the radio, but all I could catch was the word MAGENTA.

I needed to let the team know I couldn't stay here and that I wasn't able to hear the comms. The sound of the crowd was now so loud it was obvious they were fighting. Less than ten metres away from me punches were flying, some landing. The police would handle this as they always did, so I wasn't concerned for my safety. I *was* worried about missing MAGENTA STOAT. I was desperate not to let the team down and would do whatever it took. The success of the operation was always paramount for me, plus the need to get every last bit of intelligence for the officers back at Thames House.

As I started to transmit, trying to shield myself from the noise, the first kick landed straight in the middle of my thigh. 'FUCKER!' The quads in my left leg instantly went dead as I turned to face the onslaught. As my vision filled with a sea of rabid people and police trying to intervene with batons I caught a glimpse of the stadium exit, with MAGENTA STOAT smiling as he walked out. Fuck, I needed to get away from this crowd but they were pinning me into the corner.

I couldn't transmit. I kept catching glimpses of MAGENTA STOAT, now standing at the exit. I couldn't work out if he was with anyone but it was definitely him, he was watching this massive fight unfold. The police were still trying to rip people out of the crowd, which was still intent on fighting and avoiding being herded further into this brick pen for idiots. The police horses were keeping us contained, at least a hundred so-called men unable to do anything except back away from the police, pressing everyone behind them – myself included – against the brick walls. I could see the odd metal baton coming down on arms and legs, enabling the police to pull the ringleaders out.

Struggling to maintain my personal space, catching a stray elbow on the top of my head, I was faced with a decision: fight my way out or lose the target. If I fought I was almost certainly going to lose the ability to keep eyes on the exit.

If I stayed put I might get hurt. But the team needed me here. My job was to watch the target and identify any contacts he made. I had to stay put. I was trying to transmit the emergency signal over the radio to tell my team I was in trouble when I saw a shiny metal pole careering towards my face. Forcing my arms up to act as a shield, I had no idea if my signal got out – I couldn't hear anything over the noise.

The metal pole hit me on the arm but luckily it was just one blow and I couldn't see anyone nearby wielding it. The pain was intense, but instantly forgotten. I had to get out of there. Moving my arms away from my face, I caught a glimpse of MAGENTA STOAT turning to someone behind him with his arm outstretched. I needed to see who this contact was, but the crowd was being compressed even tighter and I was pinned against the wall by a wave of people, the air knocked out of my lungs.

I tried to shout for help, but it was no use. No one could hear me. I've never felt as helpless as I did right then. Through the bodies and police horses I caught another snapshot of MAGENTA STOAT shaking hands with a man wearing a red jacket with a fur hood. Distinctive, this was good. I needed to get this out to the team so we could find out who he was but I still couldn't breathe properly. I dropped to the floor, where finally I had the space to draw a breath, and at last I got my chance to send the message.

'Red coat, fur hood, contact!'

9

DEAD DROP

I was still on my hands and knees when the noise of the crowd increased to its loudest level yet. One young lad fell in front of me, looking frightened.

I don't have a high IQ, nor am I some mechanical genius. I'm not funny or the person people gravitate towards at a party. I'm no good at sports and most people probably think I'm a bit of a prick and far too serious but when my time runs out I'll know I'll have done all I could to help keep people safe. The young lad was crying. I made the decision to protect him, whoever he was. I needed to do my best to get him out of there.

I was pulling him towards me when the sound of the fighting and abuse hurled at the police changed to screams for help. The crowd suddenly ripped apart and I could see the giant legs of a horse in front of me. The horse immediately backtracked to let a handful of riot police rush in, carving a path with their shields to get to the boy.

With space opening up, most of the crowd took the opportunity to run, fearing they were about to be arrested. The rush of fresh air was like a wave of life suddenly pouring in to rescue me. I caught the eye of one of the uniformed riot police – a sergeant going by the rank slide on his uniform. I needed to play this right so I could get back with my team. I knew the police would have one priority here, to keep people safe and stop anyone coming to harm.

'This man needs a medic, quick,' I called out.

The sergeant started directing his officers to create a space around us. I stood up, allowing a paramedic to get close and examine this teenager; he was breathing but seemed out of it.

'Are you his friend? Can you tell me what happened?' the sergeant asked.

'I was on my break, I work at the hotel here. Just having a fag and everyone started fighting. I couldn't get out and then this lad fell on the floor next to me. He's scared but I think he'll be OK.'

Fuck, this was taking too long, I needed an out.

'We've got blankets in reception, shall I go and get some to keep him warm?'

'Yes please, that would be great,' the paramedic jumped in, while the police sergeant nodded approval.

I glanced over at the Shed End exit. No sign of MAGENTA STOAT or this red coat. Bollocks. The crowd had almost all dispersed, with a few people being led away to riot vans in handcuffs. Time to get back on task. Moving around the wall of the hotel building and through the lobby doors I heard the transmissions of my team again.

'*Yeah, that's him continuing west on Fulham Road at the junction of Waterford Road.*'

Man, I hoped this was our contact. Pulling my dark-blue hoody off, I realized my arm was hurting. Didn't matter – I'm going to change my profile now and just keep the grey long sleeved T-shirt on until I got back to my car.

'Zero Six is back with.'

'Roger that, Zero Six. We are with this contact you had with MAGENTA STOAT. Blue Team has come in to take control of MAGENTA STOAT.'

'Roger that.'

Thank God, it had been worth it. I had no idea how significant or not this guy in the red coat was but right now I didn't care. It was worth enduring that pain for the team. I left the hotel minus any blankets – the teenager had paramedics all around him now, he had everything he needed, and I had to get back to my job. I could have done with getting off the street though.

'Control, permission?' Given the scale of this operation, I was scrupulous about getting permission to break into the running commentary.

'Eight Six, go ahead. Target still westbound on the south side.'

'Roger, thank you. Team Leader, is it OK if I get back to my car?'

'Team Leader yes, that's fine mate. Can you hold further westbound?'

'Roger. Thank you, Eight Six, back to you.'

Instantly my phone started ringing, it was Graeme: 'Tom, you OK mate?'

'Yes and no, I'll be OK once I get back to my car. I got

caught up in the crowds outside the stadium and couldn't make my way out.'

My playful tone wasn't fooling him.

'How badly are you hurt? Be honest.'

I wanted to hide my vulnerabilities. The team and success of that day's objectives were paramount. 'I'm fine, just bruised arms and a few scrapes, that's all. Honest. I just need to get away from the stadium and back to the team.'

It hurt just to keep my phone held up to my ear. The adrenaline that normally masks pain had worn off and I knew the next few hours were going to be tough. Walking through the crowds still arriving for the game, I listened for the commentary on the radio.

It was a relief to turn down the side street and get into my car. I was cold, so I sat listening to the guys on foot following the contact of MAGENTA STOAT while I waited for the car to warm up. Ideally I would avoid sitting with the engine running, but there were still people everywhere and fans being dropped off so I didn't stand out. I could take a few minutes but no longer.

I needed to get back with the move to make sure the team leader had everyone in position. Blocking out the pain in my arms, I navigated the car through traffic, avoiding the fans walking in the road, towards my position further to the west.

'*Stations, target now at the junction of Fulham Road and Harwood Road from Eight Six. Looking at his watch now, looking back on his route.*'

'*Roger that, Eight Six. Stations, close in please. Base confirm MAGENTA STOAT is still under control inside the stadium.*'

Subtle changes in the way someone acts or moves indicate a change in intention. This contact was starting to look like he was on a schedule.

'*Stations from Base, NEGATIVE. MAGENTA STOAT is not inside the stadium and is NOT under control, stations. He became unsighted before Blue Team could take control. MAGENTA STOAT is running free.*'

The current number-one threat to British security was no longer under surveillance. This was going bad, fast.

Every operator in the team, whether in their vehicle or on foot, acknowledged the last transmission from Thames House ops room. It was the quickest cascade of replies I've ever experienced, ending with the Team Leader. '*Roger, stations, keep the last in mind and do what we do.*'

It would have been easy to panic at this point, perhaps even pile in with an arrest team to lift the contact we were following, but what would be the benefit of either? Intelligence gathering is knowing when you've reached the tipping point between getting high value intelligence and people starting to get hurt. The trade-off. The one thing we could make sure stayed consistent in this roulette wheel was our ability. We knew how to do what we do. So we do that. Simple.

'*From Eight Six, target is now walking south onto Erin Close, runs parallel with Harwood Road. I believe this is the northern entrance to Eel Brook Common. Can anyone else take control?*'

I was close to Eel Brook Common, which was a large open

park nestled in amongst the surrounding London houses, but Fatima beat me to it on the net. '*Nine Nine can, let him run.*'

'*Roger, thanks Nine Nine, easy lock on, still has this red jacket and fur hood. One zero metres from the entrance of the park now. All yours.*'

'*Roger and have seen, Nine Nine has control of this target. Base can we have a target name for him please? Just in case this target meets another contact.*'

Fatima was absolutely right requesting this, and it was better to ask for it now rather than trying to get a name for the target when all hell was breaking loose.

Nothing from Base. Everyone else was quiet on the net waiting for Base to reply, the seconds ticking by with painful slowness.

'Nine Nine, you are going out, mate.' Sending Fatima the quick message, I parked up to the south-west of the park. There was a boundary of trees but I had sight of a path leading out of the bottom of the park back onto a busy road.

Other members of the team were also positioning themselves, surrounding Fatima and this unnamed target both close in and further out, a combination of staying out of view and hiding in plain sight.

Despite MAGENTA STOAT not being under control, the team were loving this, constantly handing over control, aware of the threat level, knowing Blue Team was also in the area hunting MAGENTA STOAT.

'*Nine Nine, Team Leader, can I get someone with a camera in there securely? I need pictures of this target.*'

'*Yes yes, to the south-west corner of the park, plenty of cover and you'd get him face on if you're quick.*'

My corner. Before my team leader got onto the net asking for anyone to assist I was out with my camera kit. 'Zero Six has that corner now, attempting video, Base acknowledge?'

I could make out the red coat of the target, but had no idea where Fatima was. That was good. If I couldn't see her, no one else could.

'*From Base, yes we have feed, waiting for target visual.*'

This was the tricky part. I'd just walked into the park but I now needed purpose. The pop-up coffee and pastry cabin was perfect.

'Base, Zero Six. I'm going to zoom in fully.'

Sliding my hand into my satchel-style bag, I knew where the zoom button was. We do this stuff all the time, it's second nature. Once I was confident the camera was fully zoomed in I joined the queue to get a coffee. A mum and two small children were in front of me, waiting for their latte and juices.

Counting through some change while pretending to look at the coffee prices, I used the inside of my left elbow to slowly move the bag.

This wasn't an exact science, trial and error is how we get this right; the big variable here was the moving target. Scratching my left shoulder, ignoring the twinge from my arm, I pulled the shoulder strap to elevate the camera slightly, slowly trying to move it with a minimal amount of pressure.

Edging it up, I was desperate to hold it at the right angle. I was near enough to the coffee counter to stay in position while I ordered, without looking unnatural. For now at least. The woman serving and making the coffee, from eastern Europe judging by the accent, didn't seem to take much notice of me.

Another pretend scratch of my shoulder allowed me to pull down with even less pressure on the strap of my bag. I couldn't even feel the bag shifting now, the movement was so tiny.

I knew Thames House would be cross-referencing the image of this contact of MAGENTA STOAT. Meanwhile, I could see my coffee being made and calculated that I had ten seconds maximum before I would have to move, which would more than likely mean the target would no longer be in the picture.

Just as my coffee cup got crowned with a lid and I had to step forward and pay for it, we all got a transmission from Base, not the male voice of our operations officer on this particular day but an older woman. I didn't recognize her, but she meant business.

'It's LAST DAWN, *target in red jacket is LAST DAWN.*'

'*Roger, Nine Nine has control of LAST DAWN continuing to walk south on the east side of the park, slowly.*' Fatima didn't react to the new target name. Although this person was obviously significant, I had no idea who he was or what operation banner he'd fallen under before today. I'd never heard of him.

Graeme had, though. '*Base, Team Leader, confirm LAST DAWN? He's dead . . .*'

Walking out of the park with my coffee, I moved back

towards my car with the intention of driving away. All the while I was trying not to have any facial reaction to these last few transmissions.

'*STAND BY STAND BY, relay from Blue Team, they have control of MAGENTA STOAT towards the southern end of Eel Brook Common on a push bike. They have control.*'

The communications from Base were once again being handled by the familiar voice of our operations officer. I knew the team would be dying to know who the older woman was who passed on the target recognition message about LAST DAWN, but for now, we had a potential meeting to cover. If these two came together again inside the park then it was highly likely operational activity. Now we had two full-size MI5 surveillance teams watching two of the most wanted men in Britain in a park.

These Russian operators were sneaky fuckers. The park was a wide open area, and while you can never assume what a target might do next, if MAGENTA STOAT or LAST DAWN wanted to identify any surveillance teams they could quite easily move to a small, quiet area and see who or what came with them.

'*Base, from Team Leader, Green Team. Can I have a direct channel to Blue Team Leader please.*'

'*Yes yes, channel Eight One, Eight One.*'

'*Roger, thank you. Nine Nine back to you.*'

As Fatima gave a running commentary on LAST DAWN, who was still walking through the park, Graeme was doing his team leader bit and organizing the surveillance with Blue Team, and it happened rapidly.

'*From Nine Nine, for information, LAST DAWN is continuing south towards the rough area of the coffee place and for information, have seen MAGENTA STOAT, who has entered the park area from the south-east corner. MAGENTA STOAT has just looked at his watch on his left wrist.*'

'*Roger, thanks Nine Nine.*'

Watching my mirrors, nestled in a row of parked cars, I listened to the commentary, keeping an eye out for any known vehicles passing me. The team leaders expected a meet or dead drop of some sort between MAGENTA STOAT and the contact we now knew as LAST DAWN.

It seemed like every second things got ramped up a notch.

'*Zero Two has control of MAGENTA STOAT towards the south-west corner of the park, who has LAST DAWN?*'

Zero Two was an operator from Blue Team who I instantly recognized as Amuz, thanks to his unique twang.

Fatima replied as we all held our positions.

'*Nine Nine has control of LAST DAWN, I can control them both if they come together if you want?*'

'*Yes yes, I'll back from a distance.*'

'*Nine Nine, yes, no problem. I'll do that if they come together.*'

'*All stations from Base, quick message; if there is a vehicle move STEEL BADGE is in play, STEEL BADGE is in play throughout. Base out.*'

STEEL BADGE is the operational command that allows us to exceed the speed limits and not stop for the police or if we clip another vehicle. If required on an operation, we will drive above and beyond what is probably considered safe – all without sirens or flashing lights. But STEEL BADGE is our legal protection if we have to nudge another car out of the way or use pavements to pass traffic.

'*From Nine Nine, that's LAST DAWN now at the coffee cabin, with MAGENTA STOAT standing behind him waiting to order. Both facing south and not talking. Appears they are ordering separately.*'

'*Nine Nine, from Blue Team Leader, have they acknowledged each other in any way?*'

'*Negative.*'

'*Seven One coming in from the south-west.*'

'*Eight Two is holding to the south-east.*'

'*From Nine Nine, LAST DAWN is taking a napkin from the coffee counter. Taken something from his pocket and wrapped it inside the napkin. Napkin is still on the counter.*'

'*Seven One, roger.*'

'*Eight Two, roger.*'

Dead drop. Got to be, I thought. It's a classic move, but why do it here, this way round. It's too obvious. If LAST DAWN was going to pass something to MAGENTA STOAT why not in the privacy of the football stadium?

'*Nine Nine, from Seven One. Have seen. I'm going to see if this is a dummy run or not.*'

'*Nine Nine, roger. LAST DAWN is stood facing towards the coffee cabin counter, napkin still on the countertop.*'

Still no vehicles passing my position with registration

numbers I recognized. Crucially, no other operators from Blue Team were visible.

Seven One, a woman from Blue Team, would somehow engineer a way of discovering if the napkin held anything of significance or if it was a decoy to allow the targets to do a practice dead drop and see if anyone reacted around them. The coffee place wasn't visible from my position but whatever she decided to do I was sure Seven One would get a result. She had no choice.

It didn't take long. *'From Nine Nine, LAST DAWN has been given a cup. He's paid and walking solo east towards the south-east exit, napkin is still on the counter.'*

'From Seven One, napkin has a stone in it.'

'Nine Nine, roger. MAGENTA STOAT is now ordering and has taken the napkin off the counter and put it in his pocket.'

Suddenly the radio communications got incredibly loud.

A transmission from the operations officer back at base told us something was wrong. We had to leave immediately and make our way to a secure base in Wales. *Fuck!*

First, we all acknowledged we had heard the call on the radio.

Second, we all moved to get out of the area without making the targets aware. No wheel spinning, no sudden sprints, nothing to draw someone's eye to us. London is perfect for this, offering large groups of people you can move with and plenty of traffic.

I was already driving out of my parked position while the rest of the team were replying to say they had heard the protocol. It doesn't matter if you are in control of the most dangerous threat to this country, if the senior officers of Thames House give you this message – and this would have likely come from Assistant Director of A Branch or perhaps Director A themselves – you drop everything and covertly leave.

I knew if I headed roughly south I could get across the River Thames through Putney and keep driving towards the M25.

The adrenaline fuels you on calls like this, and you know the decision wouldn't have been taken lightly. Still scanning my mirrors, I drove away.

A couple of hours later I made it to a small but smart look- ing B & B in a village. After slowly creeping into the car park, I secured all my kit in the boot then took out some emergency cash. It's nothing like Hollywood – I wasn't picking up thou- sands of pounds in a variety of British and foreign notes. I also didn't have a stash of passports surrounded by wigs and pros- thetic noses.

No, this was real life. I had £200 in notes for a place to stay, fuel and food, secured in a plastic waterproof pouch in a com- partment within the boot. The cover story and your survival is all down to you.

I hadn't decided on my cover yet, I would have to wing it depending on who was in charge of bookings. Thankfully, as I made my way inside the warm building, which looked like a converted pub, I could see a makeshift reception desk and a woman behind it in her fifties, who instantly turned a concerned face towards me as I gently closed the door.

'Can I help you?' she said softly. 'Are you OK?'

Bingo, I thought. *This is my route in. I won't have any problems here.*

'I'm really sorry to bother you, I haven't booked a room but I was hoping you have something available, just for a night?'

'Yes of course, we have two rooms. Would you like to sit down?'

This lady had something I missed in life: humanity. That naturally occurring need to do the right, decent thing. It seemed ironic that I'd be reminded of the reason I did my job, to protect people like her, at the very moment I was running away from it.

She had clearly noticed I was looking the worse for wear. There were scratches on my hands and marks on my face from a few glancing blows that had landed during the melee at Stamford Bridge. Making my tone slightly softer and assuming a sadder posture I gave my cover story. 'I'm OK, thank you. I won't be any trouble, honestly. I just need to book a room for a night and I'll be away tomorrow.'

'Of course, it's ninety pounds for the night and breakfast is an extra ten pounds.'

'Perfect, thank you. Is cash OK, I forgot my wallet in the rush?'

Giving out little chunks of information helps support my current picture. Don't unload it all at once.

'Absolutely fine, can you just fill these details in please.'

Pulling out a booking form, she turned to get a room key for me as I took some cash out of my pocket, having left the waterproof pouch in the boot of the car.

'There you go, a hundred pounds. What time is breakfast?' As I was filling in the form with my cover name and address, I added, 'Oh, I have my car here, do I need to pay parking for that too?'

'No love, we don't charge for parking around here! Breakfast is between seven and nine and we'll also be serving food tonight, starting at six.' Leaning in with a smile, she passed me my key and said, 'Steak is really good here!'

It was like her words connected to my stomach, instantly making me hungry. I only had an hour to wait before I could sample this steak, just enough time to get sorted out.

She said one last thing to me before I made my way up the stairs. 'Are you OK? Do you need any plasters or paracetamol?'

I gave her a bit more of the cover story.

'It's really good of you, thank you. I should be OK, nothing some alcohol and food won't fix! My partner kicked me out of our flat this morning. I've been driving for hours not knowing what to do.'

'Oh dear, do you need any fresh clothes or anything like that?'

This is how I imagine my mum should have been, but wasn't. The compassion the receptionist was showing to me, despite me lying through my teeth, gave me hope I was doing the right thing sacrificing time with my family to fight alongside my team.

'No, it's fine, I managed to get a bag of clothes before he started throwing things at me. He wants me to give up my final year of medicine at university to get a "proper" job.' Shrugging my shoulders pitifully, I started to move away. 'I think I had a lucky escape from that one!'

'You really did. Go and get cleaned up, I'll have a steak dinner ready for you at six o'clock. OK love?'

'Thank you, I'll be down soon! I'm starving!'

As soon as I got into the small but warm and comfortable room, I took a quick look around – shower, bed, kettle, perfect. Before I could settle, though, I needed to get my kit bags out of the car and up here. I quickly jogged back downstairs and out of the side door leading directly onto the car park. It gave me a chance to look at the other cars here, at the B & B's surroundings, and to check if the atmosphere felt wrong.

Opening the boot, I put my camera bag inside my larger grab bag then moved back towards my room.

I knew the tortuous line of endless questions about the operation would be filling my head soon as well as the guilt from not being able to contact my wife.

Back in my room, door locked and chair against the back of it, I placed my grab bag on the soft, pale-blue blanket covering the bed, taking my black Leatherman Wave multi-tool out and placing it in my pocket. That would be my only weapon.

Then I stripped off to take stock of my injuries. I needed to wash and clean up.

10

GONE TO GROUND

I felt a million times better once I was showered, in fresh clothes, with a well-done steak and chips in front of me. Tucking into the first thing I'd eaten in hours, I absorbed the room. Who's here, how are they sitting, where are my exits and what do they lead to, what's the biggest threat to me here?

That last one was easy to answer. My own mind was the threat. As I inhaled the food in front of me with the speed of a prisoner of war, my mind was running through an endless loop of different scenarios. I focused on the final minutes before we dropped MAGENTA STOAT and LAST DAWN.

The napkin placed on the coffee counter by LAST DAWN only had a stone wrapped inside, which would suggest this was a dummy dead-drop run. Dead drops are a favourite with foreign spies, a way of passing intelligence material, equipment, instructions or money to an asset or another spy – but only when they believe it's secure to do so, i.e. when they aren't being watched by MI5, so they'll do a practice run first.

If this was a practice dead drop, then they would have likely had at least one or two more people inside the park helping them spot any potential surveillance.

That didn't explain the reasoning behind the decision to pull out of the area like we did. Had I missed something? Had we been compromised? As the lady from reception took my plate away with a kind smile, then returned with a bowl of extra chips and a wink that said, 'you look like you need this!', I continued to work it through.

OK, so we have MAGENTA STOAT, one of our highest priorities, at a football ground. I see him shake hands with the man in the red coat with the fur hood who we now know as LAST DAWN.

Hmm, LAST DAWN. I remembered the older female voice back at Thames House identifying him over the net from my video surveillance in the park. The team leader questioned Base straight away as he thought LAST DAWN was dead. I'd never heard of LAST DAWN but Graeme had been with the teams for years, nearly thirty to be exact. He would have been involved in operations way before my time.

I ploughed through the fresh bowl of thick-cut chips and downed another pint of water. I was desperate not to fall into the abyss of my mind. I was already struggling to sleep and the nightmares were getting worse, sometimes ambushing my sleep every night. I was longing to contact my family but if I was somehow found here by a hostile force, I couldn't have an electronic link to my home.

Leaving some cash on the table for my meal, I thanked the

lady and made my way quietly to my room, where I had a decision to make.

All our technical kit is either encrypted or protected, including the memory storage for our cameras. I had about a minute's worth of video footage from moving into position at the park and then of LAST DAWN while I was getting coffee. Should I delete it? I knew the live feed sent to Thames House would have been recorded too, but just in case it wasn't, I was potentially running the risk of destroying intelligence that could be vital.

For now, I decided not to hard-delete the recording. It was encrypted, and I was fairly secure, I hoped.

During our training for an event like this, we are taught to use the time to think, plan and refuel. If this has happened you're likely about to have a massive fight on your hands. Switching the TV on, I tuned straight into Sky News for any breaking stories that could be relevant to our team. Nothing seemed to fit, leaving me still in the dark.

It took a bit more effort to remove my hoody than it had to put it on an hour ago. I was starting to stiffen up and now that my body had had an extra hour to lick its wounds the bruises and cuts were really starting to show. I was fairly sure I hadn't broken any bones and was relieved it was nothing too serious, otherwise Lucy would worry when I got home.

All in all, it could have been worse and it would all heal. Physically anyway.

After packing up my grab bag and checking the windows were secure for the third time, I put the chair up against the back of the door. A metal teaspoon inside an empty glass, placed on the arm of the chair, acted as an extra warning system. I was sure I'd got away cleanly, but it was not something I could take for granted.

The last thing I wanted to do right now was succumb to the inevitability of sleep.

When you're asleep, you're not in control. More than anything, this frightened the fuck out of me. I was desperately trying to block as much as I could out of my mind. I'd learned to compartmentalize as a kid but now, after years on the frontline of a secret war to keep the country safe, my experiences were refusing to be boxed away. Even in this dark, small room, quiet apart from the odd plane flying overhead, I knew as soon as I drifted off I'd be reliving my worst memories.

Moving onto the floor, I leaned my back up against the wall, wrapping the quilt around me to keep warm and switching the small lamp on above me. No darkness. In this position I was less likely to fall into a deep sleep, and that would keep the nightmares away. I hoped. Unable to fight my eyelids any longer, I drifted off.

Gasping a lungful of air, disorientated, my arms sprang up to protect my face, sending the quilt flying up towards the lamp above me. Nightmare. Another one. My heart was racing as I struggled to focus on my surroundings. I couldn't remember what I had been dreaming about.

Checking my watch, I saw it was just after midnight. I knew from experience this was going to be a long night of horrific nightmares. It's the one thing operators in MI5 are fucking shit at, switching off! We can't do it. I haven't met anyone who works on the ground who can switch it on and off. We are recruited because we are highly observant and we're trained to take this to an obsessive level. We aren't given the tools to be able to control it. And now I was thinking about my family again. The merry-go-round of torture continued well into the early hours.

At 7 a.m., when I went downstairs for breakfast, I felt like a zombie: sleep deprived, aching where I'd been battered the day before and now stiff from my stupid anti-nightmare sleeping position on the floor. At least I had the room to myself, none of the other guests being up so early.

I wasn't sure when I would get chance to eat again so I forced down an extra round of toast and kept drinking water to hydrate. I'd be setting off soon to do what we call a fire route: an extremely long anti- and counter-surveillance route to make sure no one is following us before we arrive at our meeting point.

Wiping the breakfast from my beard and downing the last of the water, I headed back to my room and grabbed my kit before getting into the car. I had enough money to give me two full tanks of fuel and I'd probably need most of it.

Switching the car engine on, I did a quick map study. I needed to get across the south of England into the heart of Wales, west from here. But I couldn't take an obvious, direct route. I decided to drive up to Leeds via the M25 and then the M1. It would be extremely difficult for me to spot if I was being tracked on a motorway, but once I got up to the north of England I could gradually make my way towards Manchester then drop down into Chester, using the changes from fast roads to slower pedestrianized areas to try and identify any surveillance.

Traffic was light when I set off, but got heavier as the hours ticked by. I couldn't see anything suspicious but it didn't mean I was safe. Leaving Chester, I took the small ring road around the outskirts to double back on myself then drove in towards the centre near the shops again, trying to drag any hostile surveillance through with me from the fast, straight roads into slow streets surrounded by glass-fronted shops.

I was driving within the speed limit at all times, using my mirrors, making the odd stop to visit random shops, doing anything I could to blend into normal life while trying to identify those who could be hunting us.

I'd covered hundreds of miles so far and still needed to make my way into the centre of Wales. I was trying to ignore the ache I had to get home, or at least speak to my wife. *Block it out, stay on task.*

Driving away from Chester towards a small airport just over the Welsh border, I started to make my final run. Wales is almost the perfect environment to employ counter-surveillance techniques. Lots of single-lane roads running high in the hills, easy to spot if you're being followed or about to be ambushed. I remembered my last trip here, hunting extremists at their training camp. Now I was in these mountains employing the very tactics a target might use to try to evade my team. The hunter had become the hunted.

Slowly, the light started to change, the sun creeping back down below the horizon. Apart from a low-flying RAF jet screaming overhead, presumably on a training run, I hadn't come across anything that suggested I was about to get hit. So far, so good. I turned onto a narrow track, recognizing the gate towards the end. I hadn't been here since the A4 training course, but I remembered the instructor's words as I got closer: 'Always come just after first light or just before night. That way the locals don't see a massive amount of car headlights suddenly arriving in the middle of nowhere.'

I swung in and stopped by a metal gate that was surrounded by thick evergreen trees and anti-social thorn bushes. I tapped my pass against the keypad then entered a code that was unique to me. A small green LED signalled that the gate was about to draw back and let me in. I followed the driveway around a series of corners and into an old-looking warehouse which hid the ramp down to the garage underneath.

Hitting the bottom of the ramp and swinging the car around the corner, I saw that most of Blue and Green Team had already arrived. Everyone looked relaxed and was mingling. Although there is a healthy rivalry between the teams, A4 is easily the tightest department within the Security Service. Operators are told from day one that we won't be promoted. We are expected to be career operators. As such, you don't get any empire building from people, no stabbing each other in the back to get a promotion. Team leaders, and above them group leaders, were hand-picked on merit and qualifications. A4 is the weirdest but strongest family in existence.

But right now, in this underground garage in the middle of nowhere, we are under attack. Now is the time to regroup and get back out there.

A couple more cars arrived and the group leader stepped out of one alongside Alison, the briefing officer who had obviously come up from Thames House to update us all.

'Right guys, close in please so we don't have to shout,' the group leader said.

Operationally, the team leader is responsible for their team on the ground. The group leader had oversight and control of two teams and would also be on the ground but in more of a management role, coordinating big Executive Action strikes and other operations that could take priority in a matter of seconds. Essentially they play chess with us operators on the ground. They are the best of the best and most experienced by far.

My group leader, Derek, was someone I had huge respect for. An unassuming, balding man in his late fifties, he'd been with A4 since his early twenties. He'd seen and done it all. He'd forgotten more about surveillance than I was ever likely to learn. Between being recruited by Ian Grey in Northern Ireland and coming into a team belonging to Derek's group, I had followed the holy path of surveillance operators.

What I really liked about Derek was his inability to keep his thoughts to himself. He would regularly tell young intelligence officers to fuck off if he thought the teams were being asked to do something which was a waste of our time. It was probably the main reason he wasn't an Assistant Director.

I also looked up to him for his incredible memory and the fact that, no matter what happened, he never panicked.

As we closed in like a group of children listening to their teachers on a school trip, the cold night air whistled down the ramp, trying to find a way into our bones.

'Right guys, hand up if you didn't make it?' Derek started, getting a low rumble of laughter from both teams. 'We've checked you all off the list, everyone is here safe and sound.'

Derek knew this was a serious event, we all did. But what we needed right now, and he knew this as he sat on the bonnet of his car, was unflappable leadership. 'Look, you all have questions about what happened yesterday and we'll get to it so just listen for now. OK, Alison, all yours.'

Alison took half a pace forwards, a folder in her hands. 'Thanks Derek. Yesterday MAGENTA STOAT met a contact who was identified and confirmed as LAST DAWN.'

Derek didn't have to dodge the rank structure of A4 and so he asked the question on all our minds. 'Alison, LAST DAWN was identified on the net by who?'

Turning to address Derek specifically, Alison was obviously uncomfortable at giving away need-to-know intelligence, but she knew Derek would keep asking until he got his answer. 'That was Director G.'

Raised eyebrows from Derek mirrored what we were all thinking. Director G Branch being in the operations room listening and watching the live feed from my camera footage was not normal at all.

Turning back towards our semi-circle, Alison continued.

'Once it was confirmed LAST DAWN was your contact, the desk came across some intelligence, working with G Branch, to identify a potential plot involving LAST DAWN and MAGENTA STOAT. We have known for some time that MAGENTA STOAT was planning or at least trying to organize an attack on a government department. We just didn't know what or which department.'

That was why he's high priority. Take down the right part of the government and the country is wide open. The Russians think big, their aim to cause a huge amount of pain for as long as possible. Corrupting the power supply grids in order to profit from the energy they sell while simultaneously reducing our strength on the world stage, or collapsing the banking system so they can profit hugely, or disrupting the EU and our relationship with our allies.

Derek spotted the phrase that would open up the briefing further, '*Didn't* know . . .?'

Alison took a deep breath, her grip on her file tightening. She tried to relax when she realized she was standing in front of two teams of surveillance operators watching her every move, but it was too late. Clearly this was not going to be good news.

Derek stood up. 'It's important the teams know absolutely everything.'

Alison nodded, like a weight had been lifted off her shoulders. 'We thought LAST DAWN was dead, killed in Chechnya fifteen years ago. When G Branch confirmed the video footage you got in the park as definitely being him they quickly linked it to another target called TURQUOISE FLAMINGO. To cut a very long story short' – Alison pulled a small dictaphone from her pocket – 'this is an intercept we got from a mobile phone inside Eel Brook Common connected to an office in Moscow.'

Pressing play, Alison quickly tapped the volume button so we could all hear it: lots of rustling around then clearly two separate male voices, both speaking in Russian. Now I've never been fluent in Russian but I could pick up some key words in the thirty-second recording; 'secure', 'watch', 'area', 'park' and 'move', alongside the odd 'yes'.

'For those of you who don't speak Russian,' Alison said, 'the transcript is as follows, and for clarity Male 1 is in the UK, Male 2 is in Moscow and this intercept missed the first five seconds or so of the call.'

Male 1: . . . secure, yes?
Male 2: Yes.
Male 1: Start collecting now, we are all here.
Male 2: Yes. Getting everything.
Male 1: We do the practice, watch the area then move away
   from the park.
Male 2: Yes. We will see anything that moves with you.

Alison looked quickly around our teams. There was silence throughout the garage.

'When we then got some intelligence that suggested the teams could have been compromised we had to take it seriously and pull you all out. But in fact, they didn't have a lock on any of you. Your reputation is intact!' she said, trying to lighten the mood a bit.

'And their plan is?' Derek piped up.

'To plant remote access into the communications between us, Vauxhall and the West Country.'

'Cheeky bastards!' Derek stood up with a smile on his face; this was game on. The Russians, however they planned to do it, were trying to get unrestricted and hidden access to all the information shared between the three intelligence agencies here in the UK: MI5, GCHQ and MI6. Exabytes of secure intelligence shared back and forth daily, not just about the UK, but assessments and information from within Five Eyes (the intelligence-sharing alliance of Britain, Canada, Australia, New Zealand and the US), and top-secret intelligence being fed from deep-cover spies in hostile countries, including our assets in Russia.

'As you can imagine, having our comms compromised wouldn't just embarrass us politically, it would leave us wide open militarily too. We don't just share information about terrorism between the three UK services. Intelligence is a big picture.'

What Alison was saying was sinking in among the team. One of the Blue Team operators called out from the back, 'What about our team radios? Are they safe to use?'

Alison nodded confidently. 'Yes. For now. But if they manage to pull this off it would almost certainly put us back decades. The financial cost to try and recover – if we ever could – would be astronomical. The human cost is what scares us though. If that flow of information has to stop, British citizens will die as a result. If we can't talk to each other through fear of being heard, it will slow us down to a complete stop. Then there's the residual fall out of that . . .'

'Which is?' Derek kept on Alison's heels as she was forced to finish her statement.

'Once they have access to the intelligence, they can find us. You. Remember, the landscape in Russia isn't simple. This might not be Russian intelligence, it could quite likely be state-sponsored criminals. Russian intelligence wants access to a certain part of our intelligence, they back a civilian group to gain that access and provide them with the equipment and money to do so, but the SVR or FSB won't be monitoring what else this group obtain. Selling secrets, locations of operators, agent handlers, absolutely everything like that will go directly into the hands of those who can pay the most, the quickest.'

'What about our families?' The question blurts out of me before I have time to think. Heads turn towards me then instantly back to Alison and Derek as all the other operators think the same thing. Are our families at risk? The very people above all others we try to protect. Have we brought this to their doorstep?

Alison holds her hand up, saying sincerely, 'No. Everyone is fine. Look, is this bad? Yes. Very fucking bad.'

Great. Doing nothing for our confidence here, Alison.

'BUT! We identified what they are trying to do quickly.

We have other assets in this area providing overwatch, making sure no hostile surveillance is here.'

Alison didn't say who was assisting us and even though we were in and around the training areas favoured by the UK's special forces, it was more than likely we were keeping this in-house and using another surveillance team dug in around the hills to watch and monitor any activity surrounding the area.

Derek wanted to get back out on the ground. He was itching to go and it was starting to infect the rest of the team. Not one of us felt like running from this. Standing up, he got a large kit bag from the back seat of his car and was joined by two of the technical support teams.

Alison raised her voice slightly as we moved towards the tech guys, ready to get this job moving again.

'I'll give you a quick update and then you'll deploy on MAGENTA STOAT and LAST DAWN respectively. Blue Team, you'll be covering LAST DAWN. Green Team, you've got MAGENTA STOAT. We have Red Team taking on TURQUOISE FLAMINGO. The three targets are now our highest priority, making them the most dangerous people in the UK. Twenty-four-hour surveillance on all three, as you can imagine. We need to find out more about them. So anything and everything you can get.'

This is the difference between a normal intelligence-gathering agency and MI5. We could have had these guys immediately arrested and removed the problem. But what then? We couldn't prosecute them because the methods we use are secret and the directors in Thames House wouldn't want to run the risk of showing the Russians how we tracked them down if we couldn't be 100 per cent certain what they were trying to do. And arresting them would stop us identifying the real threat back in Moscow. The more we knew about them, the better equipped we would be to stop that threat permanently. We pushed the boundaries of what's normally classed as acceptable risk.

11

NIGHT VISION

I finally got a chance to talk to Lucy while driving back towards London. When you're doing this type of work, you have to memorize certain numbers, from a phone you can call in an outright emergency to access codes. The most important number for me was my wife's mobile. How many people, especially now we all have smart phones, know their own number but not their loved ones?

'Hello?' Lucy's voice told me she was expecting me to call and try to reassure her I was OK.

'It's me, sorry. How are you?'

'Yeah, all good here, I've just got little legs into bed. Any idea when you'll be back?'

Phoning home can be a killer sometimes. In the military, when you're away from your loved ones on an operational tour, you can go days and even weeks without getting a chance to phone home. Here I was in the same country, a few hours' drive away from my wife and because of the job I do, I couldn't talk openly on the phone or give Lucy and my family a straight answer.

Sometimes it felt like I was renting my role as a dad and a husband, instead of fully owning it. I wanted to be the best I could be, I wanted to inspire my family and be a strong supportive pillar for Lucy, but here I was again, choosing my team over my family. I hated myself for it.

Swallow it Tom, Lucy will detect the stressors in your voice if you don't get a grip. Take a second to compose yourself and for fuck's sake don't tell her you were hurt at a football stadium!

'Sorry, just went under a tunnel. No idea yet, I'm hoping I'll be back in the morning for breakfast. It's overrun here. I'm really sorry, Lucy.'

Working away, intending to get home and not actually managing to do it, is normal in our life. I was lucky because Lucy understood this world already. She knew I needed stability and although she could tell something really wasn't right, she didn't push it. We ended the call on a happy note and I spent the remainder of the journey feeling guilty about my pathetic attempt to be the husband and father I'd always said to myself I should be.

As the team finally made it back into London, we started to shout our positions up. We'd already been given a starting point of Maze Hill in Greenwich.

It was gone midnight and the roads were quiet. This was either going to be a sit and wait job until the next team came in to take over or an incredibly busy night. You never can tell with surveillance operations, particularly with Russian and Chinese jobs. With extremists, if the target or group of targets came out into the open early on in our deployment, we knew we had a good chance of being busy all day and night. People are creatures of habit, which is easy to take advantage of. But Russian intelligence operators are as highly trained as we are, so they know to avoid the very things we are looking for.

'Team Leader from Base, ready for quick update on Operation GIGANTIC?'

'Yes yes, everyone is in the area now.'

'Roger. Green Team, thank you for sticking with this. As you know, the other teams are out on the ground for this operation too. MAGENTA STOAT is expected to meet LAST DAWN again very soon. Although we don't have a specific date or time, intelligence we have indicates they are going to do another dummy handover in the coming hours in the area of Greenwich Park.

'We need video and imagery of MAGENTA STOAT and anyone connected to him so we can identify how they might be attempting to do a dead drop. It's our intention to let them go as far as possible with the attempt to gain access to our communications and intercept it at the last minute with our own code.'

Another reason I love British intelligence. Other countries would react completely differently to a hostile attack on the secret communications of their intelligence agencies. The Americans would likely stop the threat as soon as they became aware and double the amount of their own operations in the hostile country. The Israelis would likely go on a very lethal offensive. Other powers might bring it up in the political arena; one or two might use it as a precursor to war.

Our plan (so far at least) was to intercept the device they

would likely use to quietly observe our communications and replace the access they have with our own code, giving us a door into their own communications network while removing the route into ours. In short, quietly but brutally saying to the Russians, *Nice try, but now you've given us the last secrets you ever had.*

The briefing officer concluded with a few admin points about our expected handover times to the next team, and then Graeme took control.

'*Stations from Team Leader, we don't have a solid fix on MAGENTA STOAT yet. What I'd like is to hedge our bets – have half of the team deployed around Greenwich Park and the rest in the vehicles.*'

I would have loved to know where the intelligence for MAGENTA STOAT was coming from. I assumed it was probably G Branch or the intelligence officers on the Russian desk, as the teams out on the ground were only a small part of a very large operation. There were hundreds of people, not just within MI5 but in MI6, GCHQ and our allied agencies all around the world, who were potentially feeding into this one operation, whether they knew the full scale of it or not.

When Graeme asked for people to deploy on foot it was a mad rush for some of us to get out on the ground. There's nothing wrong with staying in your vehicle as an operator. In fact, sometimes it's harder to live your cover staying inside your vehicle because in the wrong circumstances it stands out a mile, but I always preferred to be out on foot. For me at least, it was where the fight was.

'The call signs getting positions out on foot, can you look to get a long-term position please. Team Leader out.'

Graeme was probably one of the best team leaders around, he didn't micro-manage because he knew he didn't have to. Give him another ten years and he'd be a group leader like Derek. After that, who knows.

As I walked away from my car carrying a sports-style drawstring bag containing a different coloured hoody and my video camera, I already knew the position I was going to try and take up on the south-east corner of Greenwich Park. Before I got out I'd done a quick map study of the area, looking for obvious landmarks and easy travel routes. The things you'd look for as a foreign intelligence officer in a hostile country. The things the Russians would be looking for.

I always remembered something Ian Grey told me as a fresh-faced member of the Special Operations Group that MI5 were in charge of in Northern Ireland. He was mentoring me, although at the time I didn't really know it, shaping how I should think and operate. 'Tom, the only way to truly defeat hostile forces is to think like them. Understand what they look at, realize where their strengths lie and how they can exploit our weaknesses.'

From my map study I could see that this whole area had a lot of visual 'lock-ons', the Royal Observatory building in the middle of the park being the most obvious. There were also tennis courts, a cafe and the large flower garden. But they had already done a dummy run inside a park; if the intelligence was pointing at them doing another one then it was highly likely the handover of any equipment or information would be in a park of some sorts, but if I was MAGENTA STOAT I would want to test the exit routes.

Walking to my chosen spot, under the darkness the thick midnight cloud cover was giving me, I could just see the five-way road junction on the corner of the park with a very obvious octagonal-shaped building right next to the road. Visual features like this are extremely unlikely to change and very easy to locate.

My plan was really simple: get inside the yard just before the junction, find a place to tuck myself away and let the camera start rolling. There were enough of us here to cover the whole park, despite its size and the trees that tried to obscure our view. The vehicle crews would be positioned further out so it didn't make the area seem red hot when the Russians did turn up.

Continuing to walk down a path that followed the perimeter wall of the small commercial area, I looked for a way into the yard. The main access point would presumably be a gate of some sort – vaulting it would be too noisy and in any case it was likely to have a security camera positioned on it. A quick look over my shoulder confirmed I was still alone on the street. I edged over to the left-hand side of the pavement to give myself a better run-up and exploded towards the wall on the right. As I used the grip of my trainers to propel me up high enough to grip the top of the wall with my fingers, I was instantly reminded of army assault courses during basic training. I'm not the world's tallest person, so I needed to rely on my speed and light frame to spring up.

A split second later I was on the wall, chest flat against the top to avoid creating a big dodgy silhouette. Spotting my landing point below me, I swung my legs down on the other side, lowering myself as quietly as I could. The smell of manure and animal piss instantly hit me.

This place was obviously connected to the park in some way, but to be honest I didn't care what sort of site this was, it was quiet and as long as I stuck to the edges of the walled compound I was fairly sure I could get set up in a good position without being seen. And as long as I got out before first light no one would ever know I was there.

'Stations from Team Leader, just had comms from Blue Team Leader. They have LAST DAWN with MAGENTA STOAT towards this area now, approaching from the east. If they come to the park have we got enough in position to take control of them both?'

Fuck, this was happening quicker than I thought. I had to get high, but the walls were completely solid and I couldn't climb a tree as it would compromise the whole operation if I was seen. I spotted a partially derelict brick storage building with missing roof tiles. If I could get into the roof space, I could look out onto the corner of the park. *God, I hope this is going to work!*

'Zero Six has the south-east corner,' I whispered, committing myself to being able to help.

As the rest of the team scattered around the park to find

spots to hide and the vehicle call signs started moving their positions around to make it seem like the area wasn't flooded with people, I sprinted along the perimeter wall, using the shadows for cover, quickly covering the twenty metres to the brick structure. The building was definitely used for storage. As I peeked inside, looking for a route to get up into the roof, I saw piles of rubbish, bins, the odd yard tool, brushes and a ladder. All within an open space stretching up to the eaves.

I'd already told Graeme I was ready to cover this corner. I needed to be in position in the next thirty seconds or I'd have to get on the net again and tell him I couldn't help out, which always makes you feel like you're letting the team down.

It was noticeably dark inside, which was great when it came to hiding within the shadows but it was a struggle to see exactly where I was walking. Using the ladder in the corner I extended it as quietly and swiftly as I could, leaning it right up against the main roof support directly next to a jagged hole in the tiles, a gap about twelve inches in diameter. On the other side of the small building there was a slightly smaller gap in the broken tiles but a bit higher, so I would be able to stand up on the supporting beam on that side.

Making it to the top of the ladder, I shuffled myself onto a damp, filthy wooden beam where I crouched uncomfortably.

Sliding my left arm out of the bag's shoulder straps, I swung the bag around and got my video camera out. *Don't drop the fucker, Tom!*

'*Stations from Team Leader, Blue Team have them parking their car on the pavement on the north side of Shooter's Hill. Foot crews, for information this is towards the southern end of Maze Hill.'*

That was south of me – I might be able to see the car. As I switched the camera on and listened to the dull whine of the gears in the zooming mechanism I heard Karen whisper into her radio.

'Eight Six has control of MAGENTA STOAT and LAST DAWN, exiting the vehicle now. Both have satchel-style bags on. Now walking west towards the junction with Maze Hill.'

It was a good lock on; now I knew I was looking for two figures towards the very bottom end of this road. I adjusted my position carefully to make sure the camera wasn't any-where near the hole in the roof, in case it gave me away. I was determined to get the right angle so I could help Karen out. It's quite open once you get onto Maze Hill Road at the bottom end, and there were very few people about, so if the Russians were trying to identify potential surveillance it would be quite easy.

'Team Leader, roger that, Eight Six. Base, any further update you can add?'

'Negative from Base. Nothing.'

'Roger that, stations from Team Leader, we have control over both targets now, Blue Team are iron curtain at a distance.'

As Karen gave us the commentary and Graeme confirmed Blue Team's outer position, moving out of the area ready to give us support, I held my camera steady, slowly zooming in to make sure it was the two targets I'd spotted.

It took a second for the lens to refocus but it was definitely them walking directly towards me, a couple of hundred metres away.

'Eight Six, Zero Six can if you want?'

I wasn't sure of Karen's positioning but she had to whisper her transmissions, meaning she could be close enough to the targets for help to be useful. *'Eight Six, thanks Zero Six, all yours. I'm backing.'*

'Roger, Zero Six has control of MAGENTA STOAT and LAST DAWN walking north on Maze Hill with the open grass to their left towards the junction of Charlton Way. Base, confirm imagery?'

'Base, confirmed good picture.'

Holding the camera tight on the targets, conscious of the need to keep my position secure, I used the shielding around the viewfinder to prevent my face being lit up. Although at this distance they'd be hard pushed to see anything.

'Zero Six, permission from Team Leader?'

'Go ahead, no change, still northbound, walking on Maze Hill.'

'Thanks, stations from Team Leader, with the last job in mind can we keep an eye open for TURQUOISE FLA-MINGO. Red Team haven't seen him yet. Just be aware he could be here providing counter-surveillance again.'

As everyone acknowledged Graeme's concern, I watched the two targets walk towards me. 'Base from Zero Six, LAST DAWN has his hand in his bag.' Zooming in, I was desperate to capture this on camera.

'From Zero Six, that's LAST DAWN taking something

from his bag and passing it to MAGENTA STOAT. Base confirm?'

'*Base, roger, reviewing it now.*' As the staff in the operations room were rewinding the footage from a second ago, I kept tight on them both. A flash of light burst across the pavement where they were walking, too brief for me to assess properly. *What the fuck?*

'Base from Zero Six, can you check what that flash was just now please. I'm not sure if it was a glitch in the camera or a genuine light flare?'

'*Base, roger. Reviewing.*'

'From Zero Six, MAGENTA STOAT has placed the object given to him in his right jacket pocket. For information, both wearing dark jackets on dark trousers, both with woollen hats on.'

I could feel the cold London air whistle through the gaps in the tiles as I watched them walk casually towards me in the camera's viewfinder. Because I wasn't moving I was starting to get cold. Resisting my body's need to start shivering, I held the camera lens firmly on both targets. MAGENTA STOAT had an air of arrogance about him, holding his head high and walking with a slight swagger that screamed, *I don't give a fuck!*

The next transmission was from one of the tech teams monitoring the video feed I was sending back to Thames House.

'*Zero Six from Tech Teams, that flash you saw is likely an IR laser.*'

Right. Fuck. Using a normal laser would draw attention to

their midnight stroll through the park and look highly suspicious, but an infra red laser – invisible to the naked eye – meant they were taking extra precautions to hide what they were doing.

'Roger that, thank you. That's MAGENTA STOAT and LAST DAWN continuing to walk north on Maze Hill now at the junction of Charlton Way. Eight Six, if they continue north alongside the brick wall can you briefly while I change position?'

If they continued to walk towards me I'd have to move onto the other side of the roof, where there was a smaller gap in the tiles, to be able to film them heading north.

'*Eight Six, yes yes.*' Karen was still whispering.

'Roger, thank you, and that's both targets now crossing north and continuing on Maze Hill.'

The infra-red laser LAST DAWN had given to MAGENTA STOAT was starting to get me worried. No one had control of TURQUOISE FLAMINGO and it was clear they were doing operational work. If they got concerned they were under surveillance they would just walk away clean, as per Russian operating procedure. If we got seen by these targets it would blow the entire operation.

Over the years, the Russians have become stronger, bolder and their will to extend their reach in Britain has increased. But we are winning this war against them, and it is a war.

As Karen continued to give commentary on the targets I had to make my move and quietly shift the ten metres or so across the supporting beams to the other side of the roof. If I dropped the camera it would be a disaster, so I placed it back in my drawstring bag and slowly slid my foot along the wooden beam. I knew the chances of slipping were massive but with the targets virtually parallel to the building I was hiding in, I couldn't use the ladder without the risk of making some noise. Holding onto a small wooden truss, I pulled myself up into a half crouch, which was all I had room for.

'*Stations from Team Leader, Red Team are ready to assist alongside Blue Team.*'

You can never assume a target is going to do anything – people are fucking weird at times – but this definitely felt like they were going to try something. It was our job to make sure we saw it.

Moving over the central eaves of the roof, I was thankful it was so dark, making it difficult to see anything but the cracked tiles and the beams I was balancing on. It meant I couldn't see how fucking dangerous this was. In reality though, given the dangers we face daily and potentially were facing right now with the Russians, falling to the concrete below ranked fairly low on the list of threats.

'*From Eight Six, stations, they've jumped the wall into the park, I can't go with. Zero Six can you? South-east corner.*'

Karen's whispered voice had a harshness to it. Taking the last couple of steps towards the hole in the roof, I was thankful there was space to stand up there but the gap was much smaller, no bigger than a cereal bowl in diameter. My face was still in darkness as I looked for movement to my right. Nothing.

'From Zero Six, negative.'

As quickly as I could I took the camera back out of my bag and, still keeping it far enough away from the gap so I couldn't be seen from the outside, I angled the lens down and to my right, scanning. Bingo. 'From Zero Six, I've got them walking north-west on the path in the park on the south-east corner. This is near the flower garden.'

'Team Leader, roger. Any other stations able to assist?'

I could hear five other call signs all giving their positions inside the park, scattered around. 'From Zero Six, I have control. Confirmed MAGENTA STOAT and LAST DAWN stood still on the south-east corner looking in their bags. Base confirm?'

'Base, roger, good picture this end.'

Game time. MAGENTA STOAT was the first to move. 'From Zero Six, MAGENTA STOAT has the laser in his hand, LAST DAWN is holding a scope up to his eye, looking north.'

'All foot stations acknowledge please, from Team Leader.' Graeme was absolutely on it. If LAST DAWN had a night-vision device they could potentially spot our team.

'From Zero Six, MAGENTA STOAT now has a scope up to his eye while pointing the laser with his right hand.'

'Zero Six from Base, can you tell what they are potentially looking at?'

'Negative, not yet. Give me a second to work it out.'

Base was seeing the same picture I was in my viewfinder, but I had a better appreciation of the ground, and sometimes a feeling is all you have to go on. It was eerie, watching the infra-red laser pen dart around the park finding its way past the trees till it located its target.

Fuck. The laser was still, as if it had found something they were both searching for. LAST DAWN pulled a walkie-talkie out of his bag and said something into it.

'From Zero Six, any station on foot towards the north of the park? LAST DAWN is talking into a walkie-talkie and MAGENTA STOAT is pointing the IR laser directly north through the centre of the park towards the top.'

'*Six Eight is north.*'

Mark's hushed tones also meant he was very likely in a hidden position. Moving my camera through the park, I found Mark's body outline near a tree. He looked like a homeless man, bedded down for the night. 'Roger mate, that laser is directly on you.' Just as I sent the transmission the laser swung sharply left to the west of the park and held its position. 'Stations, anyone west of the park, bottom corner towards the south?'

'*All stations from Base, pull off now. Everyone pull out of the area, Team Leader acknowledge.*'

Fuck me, not again! The Russians couldn't track our communications, they were trying to identify anyone who could be watching them. We needed to front this out.

Graeme beat me to it on the net. '*Team Leader, roger. Stations acknowledge please, foot crews first.*'

'Guys, from Zero Six, wait. I can identify where they are looking, I haven't been spotted. We can control this.'

A basic requirement of surveillance officers was that we listened to commands. I knew I shouldn't question or even override the team leader or Base, but we had a golden opportunity here to take the upper hand. There was silence, no one sending any transmissions on the net, probably waiting for Base to remind me of the pecking order. I moved the camera back onto the Russians.

'From Zero Six, LAST DAWN is on his walkie-talkie again still looking west. Laser is pointing at someone near a large rectangular building.'

'*Seven Four is west*,' Vicky said, sounding cool and confident.

'Roger that, by the rectangular building?'

'*Yes yes.*'

As dark as it was, I knew her well enough to recognize the profile as being hers. The laser held steady on her. 'Roger that, laser is pointing directly at you. If it moves away I'll give you time to vault the wall to the south, directly behind the building?'

'*Roger, thank you.*'

The strong female voice of Director G came back on our comms as Base. '*Green Team stay on these two. Zero Six, can you start guiding the team out of the park if they become identified please?*'

Fuck yeah. I love it when we are on the front foot. 'Zero Six, YES YES!'

Moving the lens back towards the Russians, I saw them swing the laser north again towards Mark. 'Seven Four, laser is off you now, you're good to go. There is a wall directly to your south about ten metres behind the building. Six Eight, laser is back on you again. LAST DAWN and MAGENTA STOAT are walking slowly north in your general direction.'

As Vicky responded the team could hear from her transmission that she was running. '*Seven Four, roger. Thanks mate, moving now.*'

Mark needed a plan. '*Six Eight, roger, there is someone approaching from the north solo.*'

'Roger that mate, MAGENTA STOAT and LAST DAWN are now static, watching your position with the scopes and talking on the walkie-talkie.'

Bollocks, this could be about to go very wrong. I found Mark's position under the tree. Zooming out slightly, I saw the person approaching him.

'Six Eight, mate, you have one male coming directly towards you from the north, behind you. Do you want any help?'

'*Base from Team Leader, put extraction strike teams on stand by please.*'

'*Base, roger. Zero Six, keep camera on Six Eight just in case please.*' Director G was backing us up, but making sure we knew we could send in the emergency extraction teams to rescue Mark if the Russians decided to step this up another level.

'*Charlie Two is complete with Seven Four.*' Vicky had been picked up by one of the vehicle crews as she made it over the wall just as Mark jumped on the net.

'*From Six Eight, negative. I'll front this out. Don't blow the operation,*' Mark whispered confidently.

I was going to witness one of two things: Mark saving the operation or Mark about to get hurt.

Holding the camera still, I quickly looked down, seeing a clear patch of floor beneath me. I could probably drop down without hurting myself too much, jump the wall and get to Mark in about twenty seconds or so if I saw things going wrong. *Mark needs you. Focus!*

'Mate, this male is about five metres from you now. Hands are empty. He's solo.'

Mark passed the covert signal to acknowledge what I'd said as he couldn't talk openly now. I watched and tried to keep breathing. The radio was silent and I could almost see everyone back at Thames House watching this on the big screen in the operations room.

Director G broke radio silence again, '*Six Eight, that's TURQUOISE FLAMINGO approaching you.*'

Zooming in to tighten up on Mark and TURQUOISE FLAMINGO, I waited. I made the decision that if I saw Mark struggling or the other two targets start to rush in I would run to help him.

TURQUOISE FLAMINGO tapped Mark's foot, which was sticking out from the old blanket he'd covered himself with. Pretending to be asleep underneath the huge tree, Mark didn't react until he received a harder kick, this time to his lower leg. Swinging his arm out, he sat up aggressively, revealing that he was wearing an old ripped jacket with an equally old woollen hat on his head. I wasn't transmitting any of this; Base were watching it live on their screens and I needed to keep the net free in case Mark decided he needed help.

TURQUOISE FLAMINGO pulled a wallet from his pocket. I could see he was saying something to Mark; it looked as if he was presenting himself as a police officer. Mark scrambled to his feet, throwing his arms about, ready for a fight. He pointed at TURQUOISE FLAMINGO and his wallet. I could hear shouting but was too far away to make out what was being said. I held the camera still. *Come on Mark, front it out.*

As Mark's body language got even more aggressive, he launched himself at TURQUOISE FLAMINGO, pushing him hard, making him stumble backwards. The target was scared, holding his hands up. Mark saw his opportunity and took his jacket off, throwing it to the floor, then held his arms out, goading TURQUOISE FLAMINGO into a fight. As he walked towards the other man, Mark threw a wild punch designed to look like he was off his face – so out of it that, given the chance, he was going to kill TURQUOISE FLAMINGO.

I knew the Russians would be watching this but I couldn't zoom the lens out just yet to see if they were going to anything. I needed Mark to be safe. Mark kicked out at TURQUOISE FLAMINGO, who turned tail and ran away. Mark shouted and jeered at him before picking up his coat. I could see on the camera he was talking to himself angrily, still living his cover.

Zooming the lens out, I caught LAST DAWN and MAGENTA STOAT looking at Mark through their scopes.

'Six Eight, from Zero Six, TURQUOISE FLAMINGO is away from you now back to the north of the park. MAGENTA STOAT and LAST DAWN are still watching you. I'll let you know when they've moved on.'

A partial transmission from Mark, as he was still living his cover, 'Yeah . . . CUN . . .'

It took a huge amount of courage for Mark to decide to fight TURQUOISE FLAMINGO instead of lying his way out of it. Not only had it kept his cover intact, it saved the operation. For now at least.

'Still watching you, mate.'

After putting his jacket on, Mark started fighting the tree, kicking and punching it. He wasn't holding back either, his knuckles would be fucked. I heard the odd scream of 'Wooden twat!' It seemed he had finally convinced the Russians. They didn't suspect this nutter of being a part of MI5. Why would you? The night brings out all sorts of crazies, and Mark was the poster child for that right now.

'From Zero Six, that's MAGENTA STOAT and LAST DAWN now walking west. LAST DAWN is looking through the scope, talking into his walkie-talkie. No longer looking at Six Eight.'

'*From Base, good job guys. Can we get eyes on TURQUOISE FLAMINGO please, we believe they are using him to identify potential surveillance in the area.*'

'*From Team Leader, anyone still north in the park able to assist while Zero Six keeps hold of these two in the south of the park?*'

'*Charlie Seven has control of TURQUOISE FLAMINGO. He's now walking north on Maze Hill going past the school to his right-hand side. He's very aware, looking at every vehicle as he passes.*'

Perimeter check. The Russians must be confident they are alone in the park, but needed to check that no surveillance teams had surrounded them on the outside.

'*From Team Leader, roger that. Vehicle crews, can you satellite around so TURQUOISE FLAMINGO doesn't catch you on the perimeter please.*'

Graeme didn't really need to tell us this, the team would naturally do it without being asked, but given the high stakes and the fact we seemed to have a director running our operation back at Thames House now, it didn't hurt to remind everyone.

'*Zero Six, you've got Nine Three and Six Nine to the north of their position in the bandstand.*'

I was watching the Russians still walking and now turning slightly north-west towards the centre of the park. They looked through their scopes again, and it wasn't long before MAGENTA STOAT spotted Jenny and David inside the bandstand.

'Roger that. Guys, MAGENTA STOAT is pointing the laser directly at you and they are static, watching through their scopes.'

I tightened the zoom again, I knew the geeks in Thames

House would want as much video evidence as possible. Jenny and David were playing the drunk couple hugging and stumbling. Jenny fitted the part perfectly, tracksuit top unzipped and falling off her shoulder, a messy side ponytail. She was trying to pull David into her for a hug, while he looked like he was too pissed to care.

The laser went dead and was put away into MAGENTA STOAT's pocket, 'For information, that's MAGENTA STOAT and LAST DAWN continuing to walk west, scopes away in their bags. Posture has changed, they seem more relaxed, walking slower.'

We might have just pulled this off. *'Charlie Seven, roger. TURQUOISE FLAMINGO has now taken a right and east walking on Westcombe Park Road. Team Leader, can we get Red Team to take this off me?'*

'Yeah, let him run Charlie Seven, Red Team Leader has confirmed they can take him on.'

If TURQUOISE FLAMINGO was moving out of the area, these two must be feeling pretty confident they were unobserved in the park now. As they continued to walk away from me the trees were starting to hinder my view. Just as I was about to transmit for help in watching them both, they stopped dead right next to what looked like a shed.

'Base, acknowledge you're getting this. It's a stop stop both outside that small building?'

'Base have seen, thank you.' It was our normal operations officer back on the net, no longer Director G.

MAGENTA STOAT reached into his bag again, taking

out a small thin object about the size of a large chocolate bar. Neither man was looking around; they felt safe here.

'From Zero Six, MAGENTA STOAT has taken something from his bag and placed it in the roof overhang of the shed.'

'Base, roger that, have seen.'

'Tech Team likewise, have seen.'

This operation was pulling in people from everywhere. We hunted the most dangerous terrorists in the world, out on the streets walking among people who were potentially about to be killed by these fucking cowards. We prevented almost all attacks and I'd always felt like we had every tool at our disposal whenever we needed it. But I'd never experienced this much input on a job.

'Zero Six from Base, are you able to watch them away if they do a reciprocal route back to their car?'

'Yes yes, but if they turn south on Maze Hill again I'll need help while I shift positions to watch them walk south.'

'Team Leader, roger that Zero Six. Stations, if they get back to the car I'm going to let Blue Team take them on and we'll stay in position here for a few hours just in case the area is being watched.'

Graeme's plan was spot on. If there were more players involved in this job that we didn't know about and they were watching this park and local streets for any movement reacting to the Russians' departure, then we'd compromise the whole job if we left straight after they did. I just needed to get out of this building before anyone turned up for work in the morning.

'Zero Six, roger, that's MAGENTA STOAT and LAST DAWN walking east, back towards the rough area where they jumped the wall.'

They were both extremely relaxed, not scanning the area and appearing to be in a natural conversation. As they approached the wall again it felt like they believed this had been a successful dead drop, whether it was a practice run or not. They thought they had gotten away with it.

'From Zero Six, they are about to vault the wall again onto Maze Hill. Can anyone assist while I change positions?'

As soon as I'd recorded their final move over the wall I slid the camera back into my bag, listening to the comms on the radio as the team took control of them. Carefully planting my feet, I worked my way backwards to the other side of the roof where the ladder was. I stayed quiet knowing the Russians were parallel to me again. It was one big game of shadows, moving in their orbit without being seen or remembered for the wrong thing.

'*Team Leader from Base, if MAGENTA STOAT and LAST DAWN get back to their vehicle we are happy for Blue Team to take them away and for your team to move out of the area once you're ready.*'

'*Team Leader, roger that and have seen. Team Leader has control of MAGENTA STOAT and LAST DAWN now south on Maze Hill past the junction of Charlton Way.*'

I hadn't made it across to the other side of the roof yet, but if they were under control and walking away from me there was very little to be gained from filming their backs unless it would help one of the team out so they could pull back slightly.

'Zero Six, roger, I'm not in a position to assist yet.'

'Team Leader, don't worry mate, I've got control. Both now still southbound walking fairly quickly to the rough turning of Shooter's Hill and the area of their car. Stations, for your information if they get into the car I'll give them away and Blue Team will take them on. We stay in position.'

It helped a lot having other teams on this too. It meant our guys living their cover in the park – Mark lying under a tree, Jenny and David in the bandstand and anyone else who was out on foot – didn't have to peel off quickly and get to their cars, which when you are living your cover is very difficult to do securely.

Still moving across the beam, I wanted to be in a position to help out in case I was needed but crucially I was thinking about getting ready to move down the ladder.

'Stations, that's both targets at the vehicle now. Wait one,' Graeme said.

'MAGENTA STOAT into driver's seat, LAST DAWN into the passenger seat, car lights on.'

'Blue Team Leader from Green Team, STAND BY STAND BY, that's the vehicle now u-turn eastbound on Shooter's Hill towards Prince of Wales Road, all yours.'

'Blue Team Leader roger, we have control.'

'Base, roger all the last. Green Team, happy for you to extract when it's secure. Base out.'

I really wanted to get down now. It's amazing once you

spend some time in the dark how much your eyes adjust. Now I'd had a break from looking into the camera's viewfinder I could see almost everything around me.

Despite the severity of this operation, now another team had control we were effectively just hiding in this area. It's much simpler and reminded me of being a kid playing hide and seek.

Living your cover doesn't stop when the targets leave the area or when another team takes over control, allowing you to go back for debrief and then home. You have to constantly think about the area, the people that live or work there all the time.

Think about your home right now, or the place you work. You would notice if a car parked up outside your house with someone sat behind the wheel, wouldn't you? Unless they had a cover – courier, taxi, pizza delivery guy, something like that. It's for that exact reason we don't make an area red-hot, because for all we know we could be working in it for years. Plus, if the locals, who have no idea MI5 are in the area, feel like something is not right then terrorists or foreign intelligence agents on the lookout for us will certainly feel it too.

Sitting on a dusty beam with my legs hanging down near the ladder, waiting for time to pass so we could start slowly extracting out of the area, I felt like a fucking gnome. The mental image prompted me to cast an imaginary fishing line. Smiling, I found a rare moment of peace amid the chaos of one of our most dangerous operations. I tried to cling onto it for as long as I could, but was immediately brought crashing back to reality when Mark transmitted that he was starting to make his move to leave the area. He'd come close to a seriously bad situation.

I wasn't smiling anymore. All I could think about was home. I wanted to get out of this fucking roof, and drive back to my family. I was seriously starting to question my place on this earth. Outside the team I had no friends at all. I think because I give off a very serious, driven vibe people mistake that for arrogance or being a bit prickly. The truth is that it didn't bother me that I didn't have friends to have a pint with or invite round for a barbecue, because I've got my family. What was bothering me now though was that I was away from them, that yet again I had made the decision that working with the team was more important than being a dad and a husband.

So there I sat, looking like a lonely fucking gnome, feeling sorry for myself and hating every part of me. One big pity party. It was just another emotional thought I'd lock away in a cupboard that was already bursting at the seams.

12

TAKING A BEATING

I'd managed to spend most of the next day with my family, doing the things every normal father and husband would do. Tidying up after breakfast, trying to make brushing my son's teeth fun for him so he continues to do it properly when he's older. Getting outside in the fresh air to play, making some lunch, tidying up again after my son had decided he wanted to make dens while at the same time playing Lego. Standing on Lego barefoot! The normality to me was incredible and I wanted to soak it up like a sponge.

I wasn't due back with the team until the morning so we had a rare night together as a family, bath time then stories, bed for my son and a quick tidy up followed by the rarest thing of all – some adult conversation with my wife in front of the TV. It was a peace I was craving and I knew my being here with my family made them happier too. Maybe I needed to think about doing something else? Maybe the world didn't revolve around the teams. After all, what was I doing all this for if I couldn't share it with the ones I love? In my heart of hearts I knew that this feeling would be gone as soon as I was back on the ground.

Drifting off to sleep in our own bed with my wife was absolutely brilliant. Perfect. I was almost looking forward to my dreams that night. I was so relaxed and happy there was no way I was going to have any nightmares about work.

It was dark, well after midnight, when I heard the most horrific scream, like an animal gasping its last breath. Springing straight out of bed, I knew this wasn't a dream, it was my son! I bolted into his bedroom, barely registering when the door handle dug into my waist and took a good chunk of skin with it. I could see my son having a full fit, absolutely rigid and convulsing fiercely.

'AMBULANCE, RING IT NOW!'

Lucy came rocketing in, phone in hand, already hitting the last nine and pressing call. I scooped up my son, and could feel his skin was clammy and red-hot to the touch as he continued to fit, his eyes rolled completely back into his head. *FUCK*. Operator mode kicked in instantly and I laid him down on his side on the soft carpet. I checked his airway as Lucy gave the details of what was happening to the emergency services operator.

Check his airway, if he's fitting it's likely he could throw up too. Keeping him on his side, supporting his head, I could see he was completely unresponsive as his tiny body shook with a violence I was struggling to support. *God, please don't let him die. Please.*

Lucy was still on the phone as she bolted downstairs to

unlock the door for the ambulance and sprinted back up with an in-ear thermometer. 'Please, be quick. I'm taking his temperature now.'

She passed me the thermometer and I held it in his ear as his convulsions started to slow. 'It's 40.1!' I knew this was bad. Lucy relayed the temperature over the phone as I realized he was going downhill fast. 'Tell them he's got cyanosis, skin has gone ash too.'

He was suffering from lack of oxygen. I checked his airway. Nothing. Rolling him onto his back I saw there was no rise and fall of his chest at all. Another check of his airway showed his tongue had relaxed and needed pulling forward. I knew I had to start breathing for him.

'We're starting mouth to mouth now, hurry up!'

Lucy was fairly calm on the phone considering, but inside I knew she would be a wreck. *Don't think about that now. Come on, little buddy.* One quick breath, a rescue breath we call it, and his chest rose, instantly followed by a huge cry, the sort of cry that young children give when they've really hurt themselves or are deeply upset. It was the single best thing I could have heard at that point. He was breathing.

At that moment time the paramedics shouted hello and raced upstairs to join us in my son's bedroom. 'Ah, that's a good sound to hear, are you mum and dad?'

The paramedic was incredibly good as he assessed the situation, kneeling down to look at my son who was now cradled in my arms. My son gazed at the faces staring back at him, wondering what all the fuss was about.

'Tell me what happened, Dad.' The paramedic started to do his obs while I gave him a break down.

'No allergies or history of fitting, fit and well. We woke up about four minutes ago when he let out a huge scream. Came straight in and he was in a full fit, temperature was 40.1 from his ear. The fitting slowed down after three minutes and he showed strong signs of cyanosis and ashen skin.'

Giving the paramedic a moment to listen to my son's lungs, I continued, 'His airway was blocked by a relaxed tongue and there was no rise and fall in his chest, I pulled his tongue forward and gave a rescue breath which immediately brought him round, and you arrived just at that point.'

'OK, while he's awake and clearly has healthy lungs judging by his crying, we still need to get him straight in, OK?' The paramedic looked towards Lucy, 'Do you want to travel with us in the ambulance, Mum?'

'Yes, I'll just get some clothes for him.'

'Lucy, bag behind the door, one for you, one for little legs.'

Having grab bags ready to go might seem extreme to some people, but it's something we'd always done. Better to have it and not need it than need it and not have it. Clothes, phone charger, bottle of water, spare change, couple of snack bars.

'I'll follow you in the car.' Passing my son over to Lucy, I threw some clothes on quickly and was jumping into my team car as Lucy climbed into the back of the ambulance that was waiting outside.

The drive from our house to the hospital wasn't that long, but you did have to cross some awkward junctions in which traffic could be hard to pass even with flashing blue lights. I wasn't about to take that chance and overtook the ambulance as soon as possible, blocking each side junction to allow the ambulance free passage at every opportunity. The last one was a roundabout which cars tended to fly around despite it being partially blind – you couldn't see all the exits or cars coming onto it. With the flashing blue lights of the ambulance behind me I hit the brakes hard and put my hazards on just to the right of the roundabout.

I was met with the sight of a police car. The driver immediately recognized the blocking procedure, tied my car to the ambulance's blue lights and put his blues on as well. As the ambulance moved past with my wife and son on board I nodded my thanks to the police officer holding traffic back and made my way past the ambulance again towards the hospital. I knew I still had to park up and wanted to meet Lucy outside A & E. Bursting the red lights, I got to the car park, almost ripping the ticket out of the machine as I entered.

The ambulance pulled up as I ran towards the A & E entrance. I was there in time to help Lucy get down the drop step as she cradled our son, who was now incredibly sleepy. The energy his little body used up during the violent fit must have been massive.

The triage nurse saw us straight away and led us into a private room with the paramedic, who was still giving him the information he needed. As the nurse, and then a doctor, started to check on my son, I saw the paramedic getting ready to leave and went to shake his hand and thank him.

'Where did you two have your training?' he asked. He saw the confusion on my face. 'It was calm when I arrived and you reeled off exactly what I needed to know. Most parents are beyond hysterical in these situations. Especially when performing mouth to mouth.'

I hadn't thought about it. Lucy had overheard the conversation and her eyes flicked towards me, knowing I would be giving a cover story.

'Oh, we both did this first responder course with the local college when Lucy was pregnant. Never thought we'd actually need to use it though! Thanks again for everything.'

As he went I was pleased the ambulance driver wasn't with him, as he might well be curious about where I'd learned to block traffic the way I had.

My son was looking fine now, his face full of colour, his eyelids heavy as he drifted off on Lucy's lap. The doctor left us for a few minutes, giving us time to take in what had just happened.

'What do you think it was?' I asked.

Lucy was too tired to respond to me properly.

Hours went by as Lucy lay on the hospital bed with our son, both getting some sleep. I sat on a hard plastic chair and watched for the slightest twitch from my son as we waited for the initial test results to come back. It was nearly 5 a.m. before the doctor came back in. We went into the corridor so we didn't wake Lucy and our boy up.

'I'm fairly confident your son had something called a febrile convulsion. He's not epileptic. Normally when a young child can't control their temperature properly the body will go into a fit. The fit acts as a quick reboot for the body to bring the temperature down quickly. What your son experienced is in line with that, but he obviously needed your help in the rebooting aspect of it.

'In almost all cases he will grow out of this by the time he's five, six years old,' the doctor went on. 'We'd like to keep you in for a bit longer and then you can go home. But he is OK, no lasting damage at all, he'll just be very tired.'

Walking back into the room, I saw Lucy was awake but lying still so she didn't disturb our son. I told her what the doctor had said. Both of us were outwardly calm, trying to process what it meant. But all I kept thinking was that my son could have died if he hadn't got the rescue breath to bring him back round.

A few days later I was driving into the garages, back on the Russian job. The sun had already set and the rain was coming down hard. Pedestrians were making their way home with their heads low, cowering away from the weather.

Traffic was still fairly heavy but I wasn't in a rush as I still had a couple of hours before we were expected to be on the ground. I had to get a piece of kit from Ryan, our biker, for tonight's job. He wasn't deploying with us as his brother was getting married in the morning. I'd agreed to meet him at his local gym for the handover.

Pulling up outside a side-street gym on the outskirts of London, I saw that part of the sign outside had been damaged and one heavy security door acted as the entrance. It would be fair to say this wasn't the sort of place that charged a high monthly subscription and I was confident that the kit inside wouldn't be shiny or brand new. But a gym doesn't need to be, does it? Sometimes, especially if you do the work we do, you just need to escape.

Killing the engine and the lights on the car, I sat for a second, watching my mirrors, checking out the end of this little street. This one door was the only exit for the gym unless it had an internal door leading into one of the buildings on either side. Just because I was meeting my mate outside of work, doesn't mean I would switch off.

When I opened the car door, I didn't create any more light than needed. I'd set the internal centre light not to illuminate when the door opened – it's an old habit but one that's always stuck with me. No point shining a spotlight on yourself, telling everyone you're about to leave the car. As I always do when possible, I locked the car with the key rather than the remote central locking, which avoided having the indicators flash.

Pushing the heavy battered door of the gym open, I could already hear people training. It sounded like a boxing gym, the thunk of leather gloves hitting pads and bags, the odd shout and grunt. There was a smell of stale sweat trying to escape through the open door, almost like the gym was desperate for some fresh air.

I could see Ryan in one of two octagon-style cages. I had no idea he did mixed martial arts. It made sense though – most of us did some form of high-level fitness training on our down time. I always liked ultra distance running; it's hard to think about work or anything else when you are out in the hills.

There were a couple of guys and a woman doing some light sparring and being taught holds and grappling on the outside edges of the gym. The main action was around Ryan's cage though.

A quick look at my watch told me I still had plenty of time, so I leaned against the wall and waited for Ryan to finish sparring just as a guy who resembled the Hulk wandered over.

'Can I help you, mate?'

'Yeah, sorry, I'm just waiting for my mate to finish up. It's pissing down outside. Is it all right if I wait here for him?'

His battered face turned into a smile. 'No worries.'

This was a basic, raw fighters' gym. The owner hadn't bothered to plaster the walls or replace the old strip lights that were hanging down off the ceiling. Silver duct tape patched up the punch bags.

There weren't any flash TV screens showing music videos or running Sky News feeds. If you were here you were training. Although, watching Ryan, who still hadn't seen me, it looked like this was another level of training entirely. He was getting the shit kicked out of him, clearly mismatched on size and ability.

Ryan could obviously fight and he moved well, both standing and when his sparring partner took him to the floor, but neither were pulling their punches or kicks . . . or elbows! If this hadn't been taking place in a gym, with an instructor of some sort inside the cage with Ryan, I'd be trying to get in there to help him. Every punch or kick Ryan threw out resulted in him getting hit much harder by his monstrously huge opponent.

I could see the blood pooling in Ryan's mouth; it looked like the inside of his lip had been split. As he pushed himself up off the canvas, the guy he was fighting cast a puzzled look at the spectators, everyone wondering why Ryan wouldn't stay down. It was brutal to watch. Ryan was being driven by something. I could tell he felt the pain every time a knee piled into his stomach or an elbow crashed into his body. But he kept coming back for more. He was hypnotized by the pain, being pulled towards it like it was a huge magnet.

Ryan was on the floor again when his sparring partner decided he'd had enough and left the cage to grab some water and hit the bags for a bit. He shook his head, utterly confused. I pushed myself away from the wall, expecting Ryan to leave the cage too so I could get the kit from him and get out of there. But a smaller, much leaner fighter jumped in to spar with Ryan. His new opponent looked sharp and fast and it didn't take long for Ryan to be on the receiving end of more punishment.

This was starting to look dangerous. Yes, there was a training coach in the cage with them, but this wasn't a refereed match. I walked slowly towards Ryan and the acrobatic ninja kicking seven bells out of him. Hit after hit rained down on him until Ryan's opponent started to tire. Not sure this was right, he looked at the instructor and gestured to ask if Ryan was still fit to continue.

Blood was pouring from Ryan's face and he was losing control of his legs. He was staggering, bleeding but beckoning for more. The instructor decided Ryan had had enough, and I walked more purposefully towards the cage. Maybe if he saw me he'd call it a day.

'FIGHT ME!' Ryan spat his gum shield out, spraying blood. He started stalking the cage walls looking for people to fight him, still shouting. The instructor left him to it but thankfully, Ryan finally noticed me. Sinking to his knees in the middle of the cage, he started to sob. The gym owner with the mangled face walked over and handed me a towel.

'Kid has got heart,' he said, nodding towards Ryan. 'But there is something wrong there.'

Looking at Ryan, whose face was covered in blood, tears and snot, I knew this guy was right. Wanting this sort of punishment was worrying. As one of our bikers he should have the ability to deal with adrenaline and its effects, but maybe he was looking to replace that rush in his downtime?

'I'll clean him up and get out of your way.'

'Take as long as you want. Every person in here is fighting for something or getting hit to forget something. It's just who we are.'

Fuck. I wasn't expecting the Hulk to be so philosophical, but when you break it down like that he was probably right.

The canvas of the cage was at chest height and all I could seem to focus on was the amount of blood and body fluids all over the floor. At least Ryan was starting to calm himself. The sobbing had stopped but his head was still bowed. I'd never seen him like this before, totally vulnerable. If I tried to be sympathetic it could send him on a spiral, but equally if he didn't talk to someone he trusted he could fall deeper into the darkness he was obviously struggling with.

'Come on, you dick, I need to get going.'

Trying to be light-hearted was a risk but it worked. Ryan didn't want to feel like a victim, and I didn't want to come across as fake or patronizing. Struggling to his feet, he shuffled over. I could quite clearly see the deep, wide cut on the inside of his lip and a smaller one on his right eyebrow. Welts were developing on his cheekbones.

'Fucking hell, mate. Can't you take up fishing instead?'

That got a smile out of him, which made me feel bad because it immediately sparked pain in his lip. I passed him the towel, which instantly stained deep red from his face, then followed him as he hobbled to the side of the gym and his kit bag. I wasn't really sure how to play this. Do I ignore what I just saw, ignore him screaming for someone to fight then collapsing into pure despair? Do I try and take the piss out of him in the hope he opens up and talks to me? Or do I just be honest with him? Honest was best.

'Mate, are you OK? I don't really know what I've just seen here.' Taking a moment to look around me, I saw that the other people training in this gym weren't paying us any attention, which I found weird. Either they had seen this before from Ryan or they didn't want to know. Maybe they were used to watching people try to run away from their own thoughts here.

As he took his gloves off, then his wraps, I could see Ryan trying to decide whether or not to open up to me. Eventually he said, 'Let's go sit in your car.'

Walking out of the gym, Ryan still looked in a shit state, but he said bye to every person in there, including the owner, and knew them all by name. Everyone respected each other there.

Getting hit with a face full of rain, Ryan ran round to the passenger side of my car while I unlocked it. I drove further down the side street just so we were away from the front door of the gym, then parked. Keeping the lights off and waiting for the car to warm up, I tried to prompt Ryan.

'How long have you been coming here?'

'Whenever I can. I've tried loads of things over the years. At least getting kicked in the face keeps me fit.'

I laughed with him to lighten the atmosphere. Neither of us were good at talking about what was going on in our heads, but it felt as if Ryan almost wanted to open up even if I wasn't ready to.

'I'm done,' he said abruptly. 'I've had enough.'

Ryan dropped his head back onto the headrest and let out an exhausted breath, like he'd been holding this in for a while.

He didn't look or sound angry; it was like he'd given up. I had to get his head back in the game, not so he could operate properly in the team, but so he didn't do something stupid.

Most people wouldn't understand the relationship between

team operators within A4. Stereotypically, people within MI5 are nosey, we unconsciously seek intelligence. It's built into who we are and for the most part the stereotype holds true. But the teams on the ground, despite operating with each other day in day out, deliberately don't ask questions about each other's personal lives. If one of us were to be caught we don't want to risk compromising the other operators and putting their families at risk. The need-to-know policy really did apply to us. At the same time, spending so much time together and relying completely on each other created an incredibly close bond.

'Bro, has something happened?' I asked.

'The usual,' Ryan shrugged, as the rain attacked the windscreen even harder. Then he straightened. 'Remember the SHARP PENCIL job?'

I did remember it, I had nightmares about that too. We'd been on the target for ages (and were still following him to this day). He'd used counter-surveillance to identify the team and I'd come close to being captured and beheaded on video. I knew what Ryan was going to say but I could feel my armour starting to creep over me. I needed to protect myself here, I didn't want to relive it.

'Tom, you could have been hurt.' He was right but I didn't want to feed into his fear. Ryan continued before I had a chance to reassure him, 'Families, operators in the teams, we're all easy pickings.'

I couldn't ask too much detail about his personal life, but he'd mentioned family so maybe that's what he was thinking about. I wondered how to do this properly, then thought, *Fuck it, Ryan is an operator in Green Team, same as me. He's my brother, and yet here I am analysing him like he's an asset I need to pump for intelligence. Stop dissecting him and be a friend!*

'Ryan, bro.' Leaning forward, I caught his eye. 'Are you worried about your family? Kids?'

'Come on now. You know the rules.' He shrugged it off and I could feel him putting the barriers up. It was ironic, really, as it was exactly what I'd just done when he mentioned me nearly being taken hostage on the SHARP PENCIL job.

'Fuck that, Ryan. Don't tell me specifics, but you have got to talk to me!'

'No kids. No wife. No parents. FUCKING NO ONE!'

The tears were back, streaming down his face, and I didn't know what to say. *Come on, think, he needs you, think!*

'No one outside the teams? What about your brother, the one getting married?'

Sniffing the emotion back and wiping his eyes, he was desperate to regain some composure. 'Foster brother. I'm an only child, parents both died before my second birthday. I'm only going to this wedding for some normality. To see what real life is all about.'

Although I hadn't known this about Ryan, I wasn't particularly surprised; it was not uncommon for surveillance operators in A4 to have had a difficult childhood. We don't fit the normal profile of MI5 employees. The geeks in Thames House and the regional outposts are almost certainly highly educated, to degree level, and come from stable, mostly privileged backgrounds. They bring an incredible analytical skill set to intelligence gathering. Those of us who are operational on the ground are different. Not special, not better, but very different.

Because of the way we work, the lengths we go to, coupled with the need to constantly blend into our environment, you almost want people who have grown up with adversity, who are at home on the roughest streets of our towns and cities.

'Ryan, you know what, real life is shit! It's filled with people moaning on Facebook, watching trash on TV and using their phones to stalk people they hate on social media. It's complete bollocks!'

My anger at the way I saw people wasting their lives spilled out quicker than I expected. The smile growing across Ryan's face told me I was breaking through, but maybe I needed to give him more?

'Mate, you also have me as a brother, this team is your family. *Our* family. It's—'

Ryan cut me off.

'Tom, I'm done. Take me to Thames House, I'll come with you now. I'm handing in my notice.'

'WHAT?!'

He was not being serious. He couldn't be. Could he? Years of service put to a stop in one sentence.

'Bro, just drive. Group leader will be there tonight, I'll speak to him.' Nodding at the steering wheel and putting his seat belt on, he added, 'Come on, let's go.'

The tone of his voice was calm, considered. He knew what he wanted to do. As we drove towards central London and Thames House I started to think about Ryan and what he'd do next.

'Bro, say you do leave—'

'I am!' Ryan interrupted me mid-flow.

'OK, what are you going to do? I couldn't do anything else, this is all I know. I'm not qualified to do anything other than find bad guys doing bad shit.'

Much as I'd like to think having MI5 on your CV would open the door to any high-flying job, it's just not the reality. We can't tell anyone who we used to work for when we leave. Ryan told me he was going into private contracting, a plan he'd obviously been considering for some time. He started describing the job as I navigated through the slow traffic.

'Real time intelligence to who?' I asked. 'Black book stuff?'

'No mate, legit. Well, mostly. Anyone who's paying, mainly commercial energy companies, but also local government.'

'Ryan, what are you going to do out there? I'm presuming it's Iraq and Syria you'll be operating in?'

'Yep, and Iran, little bits and pieces in Saudi too. Surveillance and on-target reconnaissance.'

With 'on-target' reconnaissance you actually get inside a building, whereas with surveillance you're watching it from a distance, looking at routes in and out, windows, doors etc.

We spent the next hour or so talking through potential start dates, how he would most likely get in and more importantly out of the countries he would be working in without going through Turkey, which is a well-known route into the Middle East and was therefore watched by the whole intelligence community. It was like breaking down in that gym had been the moment he finally decided he had to leave, but despite his conviction and the fact he had a job offer in place, something still bugged me.

'Ryan, mate. I know you need something to change, but we keep people safe in this type of work. Why ditch that and give your skill set to some massive company? Apart from the obviously huge amounts of cash. There's got to be more than that, right?'

The lure of money can tempt most people away from their job, especially if you don't have to consider children and/or a partner, but if you're trying to escape a world filled with death, destruction and deceit, why catapult yourself into another world exactly like that? Parking up in the garages and killing the engine, I turned to ask him:

'Mate, you wouldn't run from an abuser straight into the arms of someone else who is going to abuse you. Why are you leaving the teams to go and do the same thing over there? You won't be keeping people safe. People can sleep in their beds, take their kids to school, spend the day shopping because we are there with them, protecting them.'

I was a bit heavy-handed and perhaps coming across a bit holier than thou, but the message was right. We work among the public, never being seen but watching everything, ready to rip apart the predators as they hunt the weak.

As Ryan opened the door, he seemed to be considering what I'd said.

'Tom, the team means more to me than anything else I've ever cared about.' Turning to look at me, he lowered his voice slightly. 'When my time is up, I will go out knowing the people that have killed me won't be anywhere near you or the team.'

'Bro, wait. It's all about the people at home, those are the people who need you in this team. Please.'

I hadn't realized how important Ryan was to me until this moment. Maybe it was a result of trying to be a friend to him after watching him break down in the gym. I didn't know and didn't care. I just knew it shouldn't end like this but I could see his mind was made up.

'Catch you on the flip side, brother,' was all he said, then headed for the stairs that would take him deep into Thames House and the admin department that looks after everything from our cover identities to our pay. Watching Ryan walk away, still in his bloodied gym kit looking like he'd been mugged, I knew that was the last time he'd be in a team car. Once the team and group leaders knew he was resigning they wouldn't put him on the ground. He'd spend the next few weeks sorting his paperwork out, handing kit in and taking any outstanding leave he had left.

I felt dejected as I locked my car. A set of headlights swung round and I saw my team leader, Graeme.

I walked towards his car, and realizing I had news he pulled up, lowering his window.

'Ryan's leaving the teams. He's gone to hand his notice in.'

'Fucking twat!' Pure anger was directed onto Graeme's accelerator pedal, car wheels spinning as he barrelled into an open space. Then he was out and striding towards me.

'What did he say?' Graeme was pissed; losing an operator, especially one as good as Ryan, is disruptive and unsettling to your team.

'That he has no family, no one in his life. And he's done.'

That did stop him in his tracks, although only briefly. 'Fuck's sake. OK, thanks mate, see you in the briefing room, I'll go and find Ryan.'

But whatever Graeme said, if he even did say anything, obviously had little impact, because that was the last time I saw Ryan – a combination of our team being flat out on MAGENTA STOAT and Ryan going through the clearing process of leaving MI5.

After that day's briefing, we all ran down to our cars to get out on the ground quick, no time to think about Ryan or anything else personal. We'd just been told that MAGENTA STOAT and LAST DAWN felt confident enough to go ahead and attack our communications system. The method they were about to use was incredibly advanced and complicated, but that didn't matter to our team. We were focused on finding them both and bringing in the arrest teams.

No sooner had the team gone through our radio checks than Base was straight onto us. *'All stations, MAGENTA STOAT and LAST DAWN now thought to be in the area of*

Vauxhall Cross and the southern end of the bridge, STEEL BADGE is in play.'

'Team Leader, roger. Base, can you let Six know.'

'Base, roger, doing it now.'

Fuck, most of us – including me – had gone over Lambeth Bridge or up past Westminster, but both targets were actually right near MI6 on the south side of the river. This was the first time I'd ever operated this close to Thames House or Vauxhall Cross.

The tyres on the car struggled with the speed I was taking around a roundabout. There were already members of the team coming into Vauxhall, cars, people on foot, every available asset we had to find these two before they managed to start their plan.

As we searched the area we had to be mindful of how naturally alert everyone is outside the MI6 building. It's a lot more recognizable than Thames House and stands out a mile. We knew the targets were here somewhere, but if they were hidden they could potentially be initiating the start of their plan to gain remote access to monitor our comms.

'Base, do you read Group Leader?' Derek was on the ground with us, but I hadn't seen him at the briefing and couldn't see him out here.

'Go ahead.'

Every member of this team was desperate to find MAGENTA STOAT and LAST DAWN but, just like me, they'd be listening intently to what Derek was about to say.

'I've just been speaking to a friend at Six up on the seventh floor.

Can we play these guys at their own game, make this whole place a pressure cooker and flush them out?'

'*Base, yes, we think that's a good idea. What would you like us to do here?*'

Derek outlined his plan to go overtly loud and make it clear we were looking for the targets. '*Green Team, stay hidden and cover all the routes in and out of here, including someone on the water. Bring in marked police cars with the blue lights on, lock Six down and bring their security to their access points, making them visible. At the same time drop the mobile network for this immediate area.*'

'*Base, roger that. Give us sixty seconds to set it up.*'

'*Team Leader, roger all the last. Zero Six, can you ditch your car and get down to the pier just to the west of Vauxhall Bridge? I'll have a police boat pick you up so you can light the water up.*'

'Roger that, I'll be there in three zero seconds.'

The level of coordination needed to go into this at lightning speed would be putting the operations officer and the support team to the test.

'Zero Six out on foot, can someone watch my car just south of the bridge?'

'*Team Leader will. Cheers, Zero Six.*'

Ditching the car on the main road, I ran across to the pier and could already see a police boat coming in fast.

The police boat had three armed officers on board, one piloting, one standing next to him and one in the back holding a spare life vest who was intending to greet me. The boat swung around quickly, edging into the pier, and I jumped straight on, startling the guy in the back who was obviously used to helping people aboard after they had shored up.

'Can you head back towards the bridge on the south side?'

Nodding, the pilot gunned the throttle and the boat pitched back with the power, then slowed down again within seconds as we got underneath the bridge.

'Can you shine your searchlights onto the bank below the building and underneath the bridge please?'

'No worries, what am I looking for?' The officer next to the pilot was incredibly fast and efficient at his job.

'Anything that shouldn't be there. Can we put the blue lights on too, the same as the uniform cars up top?'

By hitting the lights we were putting the pressure on from the water as well as the land. The guy in the back of the boat had put the life vest down and was using his own high-powered torch to search. Over the radios I could hear Base relaying that they were about to drop the mobile network in this immediate area.

'*Thanks Base, from Group Leader, wait for them to come to us now, we know they are here.*'

'*Zero Six from Group Leader, can you make more of an impact on the water please? Bigger, noisier.*'

No point replying, I didn't want to big time it in front of these guys, and besides, Derek and the team would see I'd heard the transmission soon.

'Can we put the sirens on too, and start doing fast patrols of this bank,' I said. 'We need it to be loud!'

'I can do loud!' said the pilot. I got the sense this police team were loving all the tearing about on the water.

Two more police cars on blue lights came flying over the bridge above us just as Derek had another suggestion: *'Can we have some foot crews down in the tube at track level just in case they try and escape down there?'* He wasn't short of volunteers.

Getting bounced about on the boat, I turned to the officer on the back who was still searching the darkness with his light. 'Can I borrow that vest please?' I had to raise my voice over the sirens. The police officers were helping us here, and making sure I stayed safe would help solidify our relationship.

'Sure.'

'Have you got a police hat too?'

'You want another boat on this?' The co-pilot clearly wanted to give us everything we needed.

'If it's available, yeah! Shouldn't be much longer now.'

The pilot yelled back, 'We're on shift handover so the crew might not be ready yet.'

The co-pilot was moving his search light with one hand and pulling his phone out with the other, to ring and check for the availability on another boat.

I was following the searchlights when the co-pilot shouted back to me, 'Eh, is this you?' He showed me his phone screen. 'No signal?'

'No, that's not us, could be the bridge maybe? Blocking the signal.' It was us.

The co-pilot and pilot exchanged a look; they knew I was

lying. Suddenly I heard one of my team running and then Jenny's words filled the radio. '*STAND BY STAND BY, I have control of MAGENTA STOAT and LAST DAWN, they are both running east of Vauxhall Grove!*'

Tapping the pilot to get his attention, and talking into his ear, I said, 'Can you take me back please, we're done. Thanks very much!'

Giving a thumbs up and a cut sign across my throat to the co-pilot and the officer in the back, I started removing my life vest, constantly adjusting my feet to cope with the speed of the boat as it pitched around back to the pier.

As it pulled in I thanked everyone and then I was out and running back towards my car.

'*From Base, Executive Action coming in now.*'

The strike team was obviously in place ready to hit the two men the moment we had control. The police cars had already moved off and Vauxhall Cross was back to its normal self, with the security teams downgrading their presence. As I sat in my car listening to the radio, I could hear Jenny updating the team. '*Executive Action has control of both MAGENTA STOAT and LAST DAWN.*'

We'd got the fuckers. A quick look at my phone screen showed that the team back in Thames House had already brought the mobile phone network back up.

'*All stations from Base, cease and withdraw back to the garages at Romeo Papa.*'

It made operational sense not to return to Thames House from here, given the level of overt pressure we had just exerted.

Despite it being late at night there were still people around – no point handing them a gift and letting them see us all drive back into Thames House.

Safely inside the off-site garages, we all stood around while Derek told us one of his stories from back in the day. Ryan should be here to hear this. I hoped he'd made the right decision leaving the teams.

Derek stopped talking as he noticed the the operations officer walking stiffly towards us.

'Great job, Greens. Treating the area as a pressure cooker worked perfectly. Get yourselves home, I'll send a team message out soon with the details of tomorrow's job.'

What?! That's it? A priority-one target had just been stopped and we didn't get to hear anything else? Graeme wanted to know more, we all did.

'Anything else on LAST DAWN or MAGENTA STOAT?'

The operations officer looked confused by the question, as if he had already told us what we needed to know. He glanced over to Derek for some back-up.

Derek, who'd been leaning against one of our cars, straightened up. 'Does it matter?' No one answered as we weren't sure whether it was a rhetorical question or not, and he was a group leader after all.

Trying to reassure us, he moved a step closer. 'Look, you guys know this is what we do. The bullshit afterwards doesn't matter to us. We find the targets given to us and pass the intelligence on. If these two have been put on a plane back to the motherland, so what? Does it affect how we hunt the next target?'

There was silence throughout the team, but the way the ops officer twitched slightly when Derek mentioned them both being sent back to the motherland was very telling.

'Guys, we don't get told the ins and outs of every target before or after for a very good reason. We've only got so much brain capacity and we need that focused on the targets we are going after. Trust me, deal with what's in front of you, nothing else. It's easier.'

Derek was right. And I was tired, hungry and just wanted to be home.

13

SERVING HIS COUNTRY

He was found lying in a pool of his own sick in a tiny flat that stank of urine and excrement. It looked like a rabid dog had been locked inside for weeks.

But it wasn't a rabid dog. It was my dad. He'd separated from my mum and was living on his own. I hadn't seen him for years, Lucy hadn't even met him, and if I'm brutally honest I didn't think about him very often. Until I got the call. I'd just pulled into my driveway, late home again, when my mobile rang.

'He's dead,' my sister said. Quite a few years older than me, she hadn't been around much during my childhood, but we stayed in touch as adults.

I was so late Lucy was already up getting breakfast ready when I walked in. I closed and double-locked the front door on autopilot. I wasn't sure how I felt.

'Tom, you OK?' Lucy could tell something wasn't quite right. I wasn't sad, nor shaken. I felt like I'd been told about an event from my past I'd managed to block out and forget. Now it was all coming back to me.

'Yeah. My dad. He was found dead late last night.'

'Oh God, Tom, I'm sorry. How? What happened? Does your sister know?'

Pushing me onto a chair at the kitchen table, giving me some water, Lucy was expecting me to be gripped by grief. Why wasn't I more upset?

'Yeah, she knows, she just rang and told me. They don't know what happened but I know. He drank himself to death. Got to be.' Realizing I was desperately thirsty, I downed the glass of water in front of me. I wasn't sure if I was dehydrated from the job or if this was an emotional response.

Lucy patiently waited for me to open up. Although I refused to talk about what I was going through with my team I didn't really feel the need to hide my real thoughts about my dad.

'He always had a problem with drink, I think because he went through some pretty bad times in the army. I remember as a kid, when he couldn't afford to buy vodka, he'd get his alcohol fix by drinking his aftershave.'

As I heard my son calling out from his bedroom, I broke off and went to see him. I was determined now more than ever that I would be the father and husband my own dad should have been if he'd ever had the help or courage to face down his demons.

The funeral took a while to arrange given that his cause of death had to be determined. It turned out that the constant drinking had weakened the muscles in his heart, causing it to explode in his chest. The way he died was horrific, but given his mental state I was relieved he was dead. Not because I hated him but because he was now at peace.

I don't feel any bitterness over the way he treated me, nor any great anger. Yes, my childhood was shit. But it made me who I am today. It wasn't my dad's fault he acted the way he did. He was clearly suffering from mental health injuries from his time in the military and the only way he could cope with that was by drinking so heavily he could no longer be held hostage by his own thoughts.

On the day of the funeral, I travelled to his home town, where the service was taking place. At the crematorium I met his brother, the only one of his siblings who came that day. My uncle looked just like my dad, with his traditional side parting, greying and receding hairline and a small thin frame. But that was where the resemblance ended: my uncle was not an alcoholic. He wasn't ever in the military.

My uncle did a double take when he saw me for the first time since I was a toddler. 'You look just like him . . .'

He was warm and sincere. A good man. Leaving him talking to my sister and a few distant relatives I'd never met before, I walked towards the back of the hearse. I could see one of my two requests had been granted. The Union Flag was placed on top of Dad's coffin, perfectly ironed with no fold creases to be seen. I could only think how proud he would be to see it there. Despite his huge faults, my dad still served this country and that should always be respected. And he tried to be a decent human being. It's hard for any of us to get it right all the time, there is no manual, and when you self-medicate with alcohol, you're going to end up in a bad place if you don't get help.

I hated funerals, because I didn't need reminding we would die, and it was sombre there.

'Now, Tom, are you going to carry the coffin in?' my uncle asked in a hushed tone.

'Yeah, but not on my own!'

My uncle burst out laughing, then cried a little. 'You are just like him, Tom. He would always make a joke of the darkness.'

Maybe that was his problem? What if I am just like my dad?

We eased his coffin out of the hearse – myself, my uncle and four other men, all strangers – and carried my dad inside the church.

Coffins aren't heavy, at least not with my dad inside. When he died he was around seven stone; the alcohol had wasted much of his muscle mass and his bones had become weaker too.

The sermon didn't last long. No one gave a eulogy.

Towards the end of the service my second request was granted and 'The Last Post' rang out, so significant for the military, serving or veterans. It was the first time in years I had stood to attention, but with my head bowed I could see in my periphery one of my dad's cousins looking at me. I couldn't tell what she was thinking but I didn't care. I wasn't standing there to impress others, or to look like a martyr; *Look at me, I've lost my dad*. I was there to pay my respects to a person who served our country, and who should have been my dad but never got the chance.

It took a while for us to get the ashes, but I made sure I was going to scatter them. I only ever remembered my dad being happy once, when he was next to the sea. Lucy and I made a trip to Portsmouth to put him to rest in the water. I'm not normally one for symbolism but despite everything I wanted to do the right thing for him.

When we arrived it was typical British weather, windy as hell and starting to drizzle. My son was bundled up in a thick coat, gloves and scarf, with his wellies on. As he skipped along the seafront I couldn't remember ever feeling that carefree as a child.

It didn't take us long to arrive at the water's edge, the wind blowing Lucy's hair across her face. Taking my dad's ashes, which were in nothing more than a sealed brown bag, I knelt down and started to pour them over the pier's edge towards the water. The very first grains of ash made it down to the waves crashing beneath me but then a stronger than normal gust of wind piled into us from a completely different direction and took nearly all of them in one big clump and slammed them onto my son's trousers.

My son was absolutely fine, oblivious to what the 'muck' that had hit him really was, and Lucy and I both burst out laughing. It should have been sombre, a time for reflection. Instead my dad decided to introduce himself to his grandson for the first time!

He always did what he wanted to do. At least now he was free of his mental prison.

14

HARD STOP

Five minutes is 300 seconds. Depending on what you are doing, that can disappear in the blink of an eye or it can be an eternity.

We'd been to Bradford many times before, normally on the hunt for Islamic extremists, ranging from the facilitators to the men and women ready to commit mass murder at the drop of a hat. Standard jobs for us. As the team waited for our target to come out, we maintained our cover within the local area. We looked like painters, builders, local chavs, business types, pregnant women, old age pensioners, matching the whole landscape of the community.

Hours and hours had passed, the team rotating around our positions making sure we fitted in. If it became quiet on the street, so did we, melting away. During rush hour or times of increased traffic, like school runs, we moved with the crowds again. I was starting to get the feeling, as the other members of the team would have been, that we weren't going to see the target today. Suddenly the radio fired up.

'*All stations from Base, SWITCH SWITCH and find*

CONGO CAT and GREEN TOWN. They are to the south of you in the area of Hall Lane.'

'Team Leader, roger that. All stations STEEL BADGE, STEEL BADGE.'

Graeme responded immediately to the recognized protocol on the net, as did everyone else in the team. Switching jobs and dropping your existing target to go and find some others isn't uncommon. CONGO CAT and GREEN TOWN were a husband and wife who were talking about potential attacks in the United States and Canada.

I had a bit of ground to cover as I was in the north of Bradford. Although it's only a small place compared to London, if Base had asked us to get hold of these two quickly, it was obviously a priority and I needed to move fast.

Approaching a red light at a crossroads, I dropped down into second gear, jabbing the accelerator to rev-match the engine and prevent the car from engine braking. There were still cars criss-crossing in front of me as I slid up on the outside of the vehicles being held at the red. I was watching both ways, mindful that no one was expecting a car to be bursting this red light, especially one that wasn't using flashing blue lights and sirens.

Picking my gap between a young mum in a people carrier and a taxi coming the opposite way, I covered the horn and got ready to flash my headlights, just in case. There was no need. I pushed the accelerator down to the floor hard, and was straight through the gap, up into third gear and away from the long queue of cars still held at red before the drivers had time to realize I'd run a red light. No fuss, no screeching tyres or upsetting the locals, just fast, progressive driving.

'*Base from Team Leader, anything further on CONGO CAT and GREEN TOWN?*'

Graeme was keen to know what we were rushing into.

'*From Base, all stations be aware that CONGO CAT and GREEN TOWN are likely to be armed and about to launch an attack. We've notified Executive Action but it's highly likely you are going to be the first to get hold of them. We still have them both on technical showing in the area of Hall Lane, page sixty-four of your map books.*'

Now we knew the reason we were going after them. Fuck.

The good thing was that the armed units of the Executive Action teams were on their way, whether that was the Police Counter Terrorism Specialist Firearms Officers (CTSFO) or military, we didn't know yet. But they weren't here yet and if CONGO CAT and GREEN TOWN were on their way to launch an attack, we knew we'd have to try and delay them somehow.

I hadn't been on these two for ages but I still remembered what they looked like, although if they were intending to attack right now it was likely CONGO CAT would have shaved his humongous beard, common when an extremist is about to launch an attack, knowing they are going to die in the process. It was a way of purifying themselves before they arrived in paradise, which is where they believed they were heading.

The radio was filled with team positions, as everyone gave their approximate time to get to Hall Lane.

Bursting another set of red lights, using the dual carriageway to weave around slow-moving traffic, I was up into fourth gear and still accelerating when I saw the road signs indicating a roundabout coming up in the distance. Just then Emma, our biker, who had come across from Red Team to replace Ryan, came screaming up behind me.

Leaving the braking point as late as possible, I saw Emma's bike filling my rear-view mirror. This would make most people nervous, having a motorbike metres away from their back bumper, especially if they were already driving at speeds well over 100 mph. Our bikers train for this exact situation, using our cars to act as a makeshift plough clearing a way through traffic.

The roundabout was approaching rapidly. I couldn't leave it any longer – braking hard, I shifted from fourth down to second to reduce the brutal forces the brake pads were coping with.

There was no one on the roundabout itself and no vehicles waiting to enter it from the other roads. I switched my right-hand indicator on to let Emma know what I was about to do. If we don't have to, we don't use indicators a lot unless it's for cover purposes (to fit in with regular traffic). Police *do* use indicators when driving at high speed, so for us, in most cases, it's better to look like a dickhead driver than a copper. Flicking my attention to the rear-view mirror I saw Emma nod her head: let's do it.

STEEL BADGE gives us a lot of extra leeway but this was probably pushing the boundaries to their limit. I checked again for any vehicles coming close to the roundabout. Nothing. Staying in second gear, I kept the throttle steady but nearly flat to the floor to make sure I got onto the roundabout and off again quickly.

Seconds count in these situations, especially when people's lives are at stake. Not driving clockwise around the massive roundabout was going to save me time when what I needed was to take the road to my right, leading west. Driving anti-clockwise, against what would be the flow of traffic, both Emma and I were on and off the roundabout in a split second and didn't meet any other vehicles head on. Sliding the car over slightly towards the pavement, I created a path for Emma to get past and make up some ground. Instantly overtaking me, she got on the radio.

'*Bravo One Zero is now south on Hall Lane, searching.*'

'Charlie Eight Two is backing.'

Trying to keep up with Emma while keeping my speed much more inconspicuous, I took the same exit on a mini roundabout, narrowly missing a parked car as the tyres on my vehicle struggled with the cornering speed.

'*Team Leader, roger. Base, anything further?*'

Graeme was still pushing Base for something more concrete to go on.

'*From Base, negative. Executive Action is now five minutes out.*'

Five minutes; 300 seconds.

I knew every operator in this team had one goal: delaying

these two long enough so that the armed strike team could deal with them before they reached their intended target.

Emma was straight onto the net. '*STAND BY STAND BY, that's CONGO CAT and GREEN TOWN walking south-west on Bowling Park Drive, CONGO CAT is black top black bottoms, clean shaven, carrying large holdall-type bag. GREEN TOWN, full black tracksuit, white trainers.*'

'Charlie Eight Two is backing, mate.'

Fuck. Bad enough that CONGO CAT had got rid of his beard but the fact his wife wasn't wearing a burqa made me even more nervous. Any change in a target's normal pattern of life is a clue they are about to do something out of the ordinary.

'*Base from Bravo One Zero, where is the strike team?*'

Emma's voice pattern was stressed, and I knew why when I caught sight of our targets walking down the pavement in the distance.

'*Four minutes out,*' Base replied almost instantly.

'*Stations from Bravo One Zero, there is a large crowd at the top of the park, CONGO CAT has just pointed towards them. About one zero zero metres ahead.*'

Shit, they would probably be at the crowd before the strike team got here.

'*From Base, that could be the start of a large anti-far-right demonstration, due to start marching from the park.*'

That's got to be their target. I moved even closer behind Emma's bike, keeping the engine revs down so the car wasn't screaming and highlighting our position to both of the targets. Then things went from bad to worse. Emma was back on the radio.

'Base, CONGO CAT has stopped and opened the bag, showing GREEN TOWN the contents. I can see from here it's definitely the butt of a weapon. Confirmed – he's given GREEN TOWN a pistol. WHERE IS THE STRIKE TEAM?'

People were about to die. The rest of the team wasn't close enough yet. Emma was right to raise her voice on the net, demanding an answer.

'From Base, strike team is six zero seconds out.'

'That's too late, they have started running towards the crowd now, CONGO CAT running with the bag south-west on Bowling Park Drive towards the large crowd on the north-west side of the park. GREEN TOWN is carrying the pistol in her right hand.'

Two armed terrorists were about to start firing into a crowd of approximately 400 people who hadn't even seen them approaching.

'Charlie Eight Two, can you close in behind me? I'm going to try and stop them.'

'Charlie Eight Two, YES YES!'

'Base, roger. Executive Action teams aware and three zero seconds out.'

Emma wove her bike through a couple of parked cars, bumped it up on the pavement and twisted the throttle hard, battling to keep the front wheel down as she rode as fast as she could towards the backs of both targets. Fuck, she was putting her life on the line here.

Emma's move was perfect. The noise from her bike was deafening and the speed at which she came gave the two targets a massive shock. They spun round, almost tripping over their feet, eyes wide. I ripped up the handbrake and dove out of the car, flinging the door open with slightly too much force so it rebounded on its hinges and hit my shoulder.

As I sprinted round the car and onto the pavement, I saw the bag had been dropped.

'PASS ME THAT!' Emma said, her voice muffled by the helmet. I grabbed it before CONGO CAT had a chance to go for it, glimpsing two shotguns and a number of large hunting knives inside. I passed it to Emma, who cradled it across her fuel tank and rode off the pavement, back onto the road and away. Two more strides and I'd taken the pistol from GREEN TOWN before her brain had a chance to process what was happening.

The Executive Action team would be here any second. I couldn't tell if GREEN TOWN had a suicide vest on under her tracksuit and I wasn't about to stick around to check.

'From Team Leader, Base, can you tell Executive Action teams that CONGO CAT and GREEN TOWN are still on Bowling Park Drive. I can guide them in if they need it.'

Graeme obviously had eyes on this and had called it in.

I ran back to the driver's side of my car, taking the opportunity to quickly scan the area to see if the noise we had just created had drawn the attention of any locals. It was a quiet residential street, but so far no one had reacted.

I climbed into the driver's seat just as my mirrors lit up with blue flashes followed by sirens, as three police vehicles from the Executive Action team came flying up the road towards me, three more approaching from behind in the distance. The car was buffeted by the rush of air from the police vehicles as they passed.

Putting the pistol on the passenger seat, I covered it up with my map book and waited for a gap in the transmissions from Graeme, who was rapidly describing what was happening with the targets.

'That's the Executive Action team on site now, from Team Leader. They have control of CONGO CAT and GREEN TOWN who are on the floor. No shots fired.'

'Roger that from Base, happy for you all to withdraw back to garages for debrief.'

'All stations from Team Leader, cease and withdraw. Acknowledge down the list please.'

'Charlie Eight Two, roger the cease. Bravo One Zero, want me to take that bag?' I'd managed to catch her up, as Emma had slowed down to avoid standing out.

'Yes yes mate, pull up alongside me here.'

As we drove to our regional outpost for debrief, Graeme popped up again on the net, already thinking ahead. *'Base from Team Leader, can we arrange for one of our friends to meet us at the garages to take custody of this bag please.'*

'Base, roger that.'

Our friends, meaning Special Branch. Whenever we have to hand evidence over we use Special Branch as our conduit to the uniformed police, as SB hold a much higher security clearance than uniform police and operate very differently too, more in line with how we work. Some of the bravest police officers I have ever met are from Special Branch in Northern Ireland.

Getting out of the car in the garages, I could see Emma already talking to the operations officer and Director A, who's in charge of our whole operational wing of MI5. Standing to the side of them was an older guy, cord trousers, strong but comfortable walking shoes, dark fleece covering a checked shirt. This was our man from Special Branch.

Holding my hand out, I said, 'Hi mate, you here for the bag of longs?'

Long is slang for rifle in the same way a *short* would be a pistol. It's more of a military term but one that would instantly make him feel relaxed and on familiar ground. Just because we are an MI5 surveillance team doesn't mean we are a bunch of big-time dickheads. We are all small cogs in a well-oiled machine and I always made the effort for Special Branch and Counter Terrorism Unit officers.

Accepting my handshake, he didn't offer his name – there was no need. The operations officer would have escorted him here, plus the few police officers that do have access to us know they are never going to get our real names, so they don't bother giving theirs.

The Special Branch guy walked over to my car and handed me a pair of latex gloves. 'You've touched them already, I take it?'

A quick breath of air into each glove and they expanded

nicely to fit over my hands without too much fuss. 'The pistol yeah, looks like an old Hi-Power. Want some help making them safe?'

'Yeah, let's see what we have first. I'll quickly photograph them and get them out of here and leave you to it.'

This guy was probably close to retirement, but despite being old enough to be my dad there was a level of respect he offered that required no words. When we encounter someone outside 'the circle', which is what we call the intelligence community (MI5, MI6, GCHQ or one of our close foreign intelligence allies) we're normally met with one of two reactions.

The most common is for people to be awkward around us, mistrusting and slightly nervous despite the best efforts of the intelligence employee they are meeting to calm and reassure them. At the other end of the scale, one or two can overcompensate *massively* to the point where their attitude is bordering on arrogance towards us, almost as if they have to prove how fucking nails they are in our presence.

That's the complete opposite of who we are, even the operators in the teams who are doing the dirty work out on the streets.

If anything, when we do deal with outside agencies, and it's not often at our level we do, we tend to make sure there is some sort of relationship built in case we need to capitalize on it at a later date.

Taking the bag out of the passenger seat and handing it to the SB officer, I picked the pistol up and followed him to the boot of my car, which now acted as a makeshift table.

Pointing the pistol in a safe direction, I did the usual checks you would do when handling any new weapon. Safety on, then drop the magazine. I placed it on the boot, pulled the working parts and went through the procedure of making the weapon completely safe, as in no round in the chamber and no magazine fitted.

'That's how you found it then?' the Special Branch officer asked.

I would expect that the state of the weapons and how they were recovered would be in the police report, but it would leave out how and who they were recovered by.

'Yeah, she had it in her hand. Everything else was in the bag,' I said.

I watched him carefully removing the knives from the bag, then a shotgun with the barrels chopped down.

'Anything else I can help with, mate?'

The Special Branch officer didn't need any more information, at least not yet, so I left him to photograph the weapons and then place everything back in the bag.

'Emma, Tom, I wanted to make sure you are both OK,' Graeme said.

'Yeah, fine,' we both said.

Graeme nodded and left to sort the others out before they headed home.

I held my hand out to shake Emma's. 'Welcome to the team!'

'See you tomorrow, mate.'

And that was the end of the conversation. We work

extremely hard on the ground so when we get a chance to go home we disappear quickly.

Door closed, phone tucked under my left thigh, clutch in, into first gear, engine switched on, I was ready to go, just waiting for the other cars to drive past and get out of the way so we didn't all leave in a tight convoy.

Man, I was so happy to be on my way home. I wanted to read a bedtime story to my son and walk into a room, any room, and actually see Lucy.

The car in front of me was almost out of the garages. I went to pull out.

Then GREEN TOWN and CONGA CAT were in front of my car, from nowhere, as the deafening roar of a motorbike filled my ears. *FUCK.*

The car lurched forward and back violently as my foot slipped off the clutch, stalling the engine. My neck snapped and the two targets disappeared from view. I stamped on the brakes. What the hell was that?

When my lungs convulsed in an attempt to get air into me, I realized I'd been holding my breath. The gasp forced me to relax my white-knuckle grip on the steering wheel.

Emma's bike was leaving the garages, the engine roar fading away.

Thankfully no one had witnessed whatever it was that had just happened to me. Starting the engine again, I had to back the car up slightly to make the corner.

How long could I keep hiding from the fact that something was seriously wrong?

15

LUCY'S STORY

Watching your husband fall apart is never easy. It's made worse when he can't talk to you about his work and won't even admit there's a problem. And you can't confide in anyone else, at least not without making up a cover story and then having to remember all your lies.

One incident sticks in my mind as being the first time I saw the physical evidence something was really wrong. We had all gone to the park and it was a normal day, nice and warm, just us in the moment. My son was messing around on the grass pulling up as many dandelions as he could and I was making sure he didn't eat any!

I turned to Tom as I laughed at the way our son was stuffing everything into his mouth. Tom's eyes were fixed to a spot on the ground in front of him. His breathing was shallow but rapid, he was holding his chest with one hand. I knew this was an extreme panic attack of sorts.

'Look at me, it's OK. Slow your breathing down, look at me.'

Holding his gaze, I slowly managed to bring him back down and get his breathing under control, while keeping an eye on my son and his determined plan to eat pickings from the grass.

All Tom would say afterwards was that he was fine now, it was nothing and it wouldn't happen again. The fear that there was something seriously wrong was starting to eat away at me.

But we carried on; I desperately tried to make sure our family was held together and most of the time it was working.

I remember the first time I set eyes on Tom on an airstrip in Northern Ireland when we were both in the military. He was standing in a protective and alert manner, waiting to escort us back to base, and there was something about him that immediately drew me.

He never got bogged down in slagging someone off, or moaning about a situation. He would just get on with what needed to be done.

It was a total whirlwind romance from our meeting each other to getting a brief bit of time off to get married. It could have gone so wrong, really, doing everything so quickly, but when you know, you know. Why waste time?

Nothing is perfect, and things change, kids come along, so every marriage needs to be worked on as we all grow older and responsibility takes hold.

Tom only started to change when he joined MI5. Being a surveillance officer was his natural calling but very early on I could see the difference in him. He would struggle to hold a full-length conversation without becoming distracted by something else. His head just wasn't in the moment with me. It was with his team.

He would go away for a week and barely text or call, and when he did he was distant. Before this, he would always text me and now I had to send him ten messages just to get one back. He came home at the weekend and would barely look at me or our son. If I tried to hold his hand it would be like holding a doorknob, if I cuddled him it was like cuddling a piece of wood, if I asked him what was wrong we would get into an argument and he would give me some bullshit excuses. Eventually he told me he just felt different. I spent days crying, waiting for calls or a text when he was away, convinced he was seeing someone else. Why else would he be so cold towards me? For weeks in between trips away I tried everything, from the soft approach to the full-on *What the fuck is the matter?!* I finally had enough and was ready to leave with our son when he rang me out of nowhere and told me he was sorry for what he had put me through and he loved me more than ever. From that day he was back to himself where our son and I were concerned; he came home and we were fine and never spoke of it again.

I'm not the perfect wife. I wasn't then, I'm certainly not now. I hate cooking, I hate endlessly cleaning up after the kids (we have two now). Some days I barely have a chance to make myself a drink, never mind tidy the house. I wanted our days to be spent in the sea, towelling the kids down after body boarding, getting warm in our hoodies with scruffy hair.

Back then sometimes I just wished the world would disappear and leave us to it. Even though Tom and I were good again I could see that something was not right with him. I was starting to hate what was happening to Tom; he was losing his energy, his love for life. I knew his job was important, not just to him but for everyone else. But was his job worth his personality? The person I married? Our family?

Tom has never told me what to do, I'd tell him to do one if he did! He doesn't want me to stay at home, nor have a career to replace what I did in the military. Tom has always said he wants me to do whatever makes me happy, which is great, I love that about him.

I started to notice the first signs of PTSD (although I didn't know it was that) when he drifted off to sleep in the living room while I was watching TV. It was nice being in the same room together, but it didn't last long. Out of nowhere he jumped up, threw the cushions off the sofa and tried to bury himself down the back of it like a cat that had just heard a firework for the first time. It frightened the life out of me and I froze. I had to wait until he stopped thrashing about before I could try to bring him round. His eyes were wild and glazed over, he was looking at me but clearly not seeing me. But as quickly as it had come it went, and his eyes returned to normal.

'What did I do?' he said. When I told him, he just looked blank.

'Fuck me, what were you trying to get away from then?' I kind of laughed in a nervous way. He didn't remember.

I love my husband, I would do anything for him. But I had no idea how to help him get through this. He wouldn't talk to me; we had normal conversations, but asking him anything about work was like getting blood from a stone. It was starting to affect family life now too.

No one on my side of the family knew anything about what Tom did for a day job. I always referred to the Security Service as 'the office'. It never raised any questions if someone overheard it. It meant I had to lie to my family and to my friends – and always will do.

I remember one night we'd managed to get to bed reasonably early after having a bit of grown-up time together. I went up first, leaving Tom to run around quietly downstairs, as he likes to have everything ready for the morning. Drifting off that night I can just about remember Tom getting into bed, being as quiet as possible.

Falling asleep with him next to me was nice.

BANG! Out of the darkness a pain shot into my eye. It was pitch black. Tom grabbed my hand; he was sweating and trembling.

'I'm sorry, Lucy, I'm so *so* sorry. I didn't mean to.'

Tom had punched me in the middle of a nightmare. The shock of hitting something must have woken him up as much as it did me.

'It's fine,' I said, as Tom tried to examine my eye. 'Get off me and fetch me some ice.'

I know he didn't mean to do it but I was so annoyed, mostly because I knew I'd never get back to sleep and I was already exhausted. By the time he came back up with an ice block wrapped in a tea towel I had calmed down a little. In the light from the bedside lamp I could see a worried look on Tom's face.

'Give that here, ya div,' I said, smiling.

I knew being mad at him was pointless and would only make him more stressed and twitchy when he slept, so we talked until we relaxed and fell back to sleep. In the morning I discovered a lovely black eye had started to develop. How the hell was I gonna explain this one?

Living with a spy wasn't a normal life. The school runs were never run of the mill, eight minutes is all it would take as traffic was never a problem. Tom was expert at getting through it, and I would sink down in the car as he would pull moves that would earn him a well-deserved beep from other drivers! We would have to take a different route to school every day, go all the way around roundabouts before taking the exit or taking four lefts to check for anyone following. When we eventually arrived at school we took our son into his class and waited in the yard until everyone had gone. We were definitely thought of as weird and over-cautious parents but we didn't care. Once the playground was empty we had to check the doors to his classroom were closed and that the entrances and exits to school were locked. Outside school we would check for anyone suspicious hanging around and any cars that looked out of place. Once what had become a ritual was complete we could leave to carry on the rest of our unconventional day.

Living with an ex-spy isn't a normal life either.

16

STARTING AGAIN

I don't know why this particular nightmare was the final straw, the moment I knew I had to seek help. Perhaps it was the fear in Lucy's eyes when I woke up huddled in the corner of the bedroom, dripping with sweat, my knuckles grazed, and no fucking idea what had just happened. I'd been feeling guilty for years about putting my job before my family, and finally I knew it had to stop.

I called MI5's Welfare Department and admitted I was having problems. The same day I was assessed by a psychiatrist and taken off the team. I never saw them again. Life as I knew it was over.

Eventually I was diagnosed with PTSD and was told that the flashbacks and the nightmares were my brain's attempt to make sense of events. I was hyper-vigilant, noticing everything – the very skills I needed in surveillance were undermining me now, as I never switched off. As a result my brain was struggling to process what I was seeing every day.

I had the very best help I could get from the Security Service, for which I'll always be grateful. I only started to come across problems in the treatment part of my recovery when I came up against NHS professionals. I love our NHS, from the porters right the way through to the doctors and nurses. The problem wasn't them being unprofessional. The issue I had was being able to trust the person I was talking to, given that they also had my home address on their system. I didn't trust anyone so I couldn't open up and talk about what was happening to me. At that point I didn't have any idea how to make sure I got back on track. I couldn't properly identify what was going wrong until I started the psychotherapy, and that couldn't start until a professional could listen to me vocalizing what was going on.

With the help of the Security Service, I found the right people I could talk to and start back on the path to recovery.

It had been a while since I'd had paid work, a normal job. The treatment phase of my PTSD was intense and while I believe you are and always will be susceptible to some sort of relapse at some point, I got to the point where I could start thinking about earning some money again. Providing for my family. Being a proper dad and husband – in my own head, what I'd always wanted to be, but felt I was missing the mark.

Borrowing a laptop from Lucy's brother, I started to write my CV, feeling fairly confident that if I could get the basic layout right, it would be enough to get me in the door of any big company. From there I could start building a new career. Being in MI5 and the military for a decade had given me some incredible personality traits and motivation, something

I was sure would land me a job paying at the same level as the Service; just under £30,000 a year, before overtime.

It wasn't long before I hit a major hurdle. What was I going to put down on paper as my previous job? Joining the army is fine, looks great. Being posted as an engineer to Germany, brilliant. Then what? I couldn't write that I was in Special Operations then MI5 as a Surveillance Operator. Fuck. We are under a lifetime restriction from telling people who we really are and what we did. The only way round the problem was to put the whole time block under the banner title of 'delivery driver'.

Finishing up the CV didn't take long, but I made it look as smart as possible and emailed it to as many local job agencies and companies as I could find. I was getting close to a hundred emails and applications over twenty-four hours of constant searching and applying. It wasn't long before I got the first call from a recruitment company. *Perfect*, I thought.

'Hi, can I speak to Tom, please?'

'Yes, speaking . . .'

Good start, pleasant, formal but approachable. This could be it.

'I'm Anna. You recently sent us your CV, is now a good time to talk?'

'Yes, definitely. Thank you so much for ringing me back!'

Waving like a mad man to Lucy, who was in the garden, I could barely hold back my excitement as she rushed in.

'Great, well my role here is to provide suitable long-term

employment to people looking for career changes, particularly those who have recently left the military.'

Anna continued to talk about her position and the job I'd initially applied for as team leader within a large logistics company. She thought I was suitable, which made sense given my cover story as a delivery driver and the fact I had gained all my driving licences within the first few years with the engineers in the army. I could pretty much drive anything, so I understood the role of drivers.

The call was going really well and the promises of secure immediate employment gave me a feeling of safety. Soon I'd be able to provide for my family. That dream came crashing down when Anna continued.

'If I'm honest, Tom, your CV does put you into a job offering straight away but not as a team leader. My clients and all big leading logistics firms all require civilian experience within that role, it's a very different environment to the military. But, there's no saying that once you're in position you can't then apply for that role. It's often easier to get the job you *really* want when you have a job.'

This was exactly what I had been afraid of. I thought I was aiming low by going for a team leader role but to be told that was still too high was hard to hear. Anna continued her attempt at reeling me in.

'I can get you into work at the beginning of next week, on the warehouse floor, temping. I take it you already have safety boots and that you're still fit and healthy?'

'Safety boots. Yeah. Got them.'

I SPY

I was completely torn. I needed the work, I needed the money. But some part of me thought I should be aiming higher.

Or should I? I was completely confident in my ability as a surveillance operator with MI5, it's who I am. Was. Up till now I had been 100 per cent sure I could bring some piece of that ability to a new career and into the civilian world. I was starting to realize that was going to be much harder than I first thought.

'So as you know, Tom, we are an agency. The company will pay us and we then pay you, we handle all your payroll, your terms of employment, absolutely everything. We take the hassle out of it all.'

Anna went on to explain that because I would be on a zero-hours contract and working via the temping agency, I would actually end up with less than minimum wage. Lucy could hear this standing next to me, and must have been able to sense my disappointment. I could see her face, smiling and full of confidence in me, as she took the phone out of my hand and hung up. Anna was saying something about setting me up on her system as the line went dead.

I knew what Lucy was going to say before she opened her mouth.

'You are starting again,' she said, smiling. 'That's fine, but start something that respects you and your ability.'

Fuck. Lucy saying this reminded me why I wanted to marry her so quickly when we first met in Northern Ireland. She

267

makes me believe there is something more to me. Putting my phone on the side, Lucy carried on:

'I don't mind you starting on minimum wage *if* you have the chance to progress. I'm not letting you go to a job which you hate if there is no chance of you running the place.'

The laughter surged out of me, instantly causing Lucy to laugh too.

'No, but listen. I know you can work up to something great. It will take time but being able to climb a ladder is better for you than being held down by a rock.'

Lucy was right, and seeing it in my mind this way made perfect sense. I wanted to be able to have something to strive for – if I couldn't put myself on the line to stop terrorists killing people then I would channel that into building a career, whatever that may be.

I went back to the laptop straight away, applying for even more jobs and hearing back from recruitment agencies as well as directly from employers. I eventually got an interview for a local IT solutions company. Some of the more experienced techs in this industry can earn a lot of money and there were a ton of courses I could do alongside work to be able to move up the ladder.

The night before the interview I got my kit ready; shirt, tie, polished shoes. I looked at my smart clothes then glanced around the upstairs of the house, which was missing its internal doors; we'd started to renovate but hadn't had the money to finish. Time to change this. Put the pain and suffering behind us and be the husband and dad Lucy believed in.

As I was going to sleep, I thought about the possible questions, the job description, how I could twist my experience to make sure it filled the gaps. Surely this interview would be easier than the selection day for MI5! Fuck, I missed the team so badly. I knew they wouldn't have time to be thinking about me, but at that moment, lying next to Lucy, I would have given anything to be part of the team again, to belong to something that mattered.

Shake it off, Tom. Need to close that door. You've worked hard to climb out of this hole. Next step is to actually prove you are *something and get on with the next challenge, with real life.*

I was awake ten minutes before my alarm went the next morning. It wasn't long before I had to make a move to get to the interview on time. I wanted to have a look at the area beforehand. I suppose it's an old habit but if you're comfortable with the building's structure on the outside it makes it a lot easier going inside and that's how I wanted to appear, comfortable and confident rather than nervous.

Lucy needed the car so I had two options for getting to the interview. A bus then a five-minute walk, or a forty-minute walk from the house. It was a clear, fairly warm morning and I could do with the clarity that any sort of exercise gives you. The last thing I needed was to relapse into hyper-vigilance and scare off the interviewer.

Trying not to focus on the vehicles passing me or everyday people on their commute to work, I played out interview scenarios in my head. But deep down I was worried about them questioning the obvious gap or cover-up in my CV.

I was walking faster than my normal pace and arrived early. There was a car park in front of the building, which was purpose built, not a converted warehouse or mill, with large tinted-glass windows. Given this was an IT solutions company it made total sense to restrict what could be seen from the outside. I was expecting a bit more security though. It was an open car park, with no barriers. Standard deterrent CCTV cameras around the outside, positioned on the corners following the lines of the building, but nothing aiming at the car park entrance.

Keep walking, you've got time. I wanted to have a solid picture of how secure the building and the area was. Heading south down the slight hill, I spotted a smoking shelter with five employees, all seeming happy but all of them with their passes showing. All five had security keys and USB stick devices attached to the lanyards. Nothing out of the ordinary in this type of work setting, I'd followed a lot of targets who had day jobs in IT. I'd keep in mind that this place obviously didn't see security as a priority. Following the hedge line which was half-covering the car park, I saw a corner shop just in front of me. This gave me the cover I needed, allowing me to go in and then come out and head back towards the entrance, better than just turning around on the street.

Chances were that no one had batted an eye at me here, but that didn't matter to me. Always blend in, never draw anyone's attention to you, for any reason. Coming out of the shop with some chewing gum, I walked towards the main doors. There was a fair bit of activity, cars and people leaving and arriving, suggesting that they had an overnight shift pattern. From the positioning of the large one-way windows to the right of the entrance, I guessed the reception was to the right.

There were employees walking over to me from the smoking shelter. Three men, two women, all in their early twenties, perhaps younger. Only one of the men was smart, the other two had their shirts untucked. Black leather shoes scuffed and unpolished. The women were smart but on the walk over from the smoking shelter they both flicked their cigarette butts into the car park rather than use the bins provided.

Using this group as cover, I took half a second to scan the area before following them inside. Keypad-protected double doors to my left led to an open-plan office housing rows and rows of people sitting in front of computers. Metal stairs in front of me with reception to my right. Behind the curved polished plastic of the reception area I could see another pad-protected door.

As the group in front of me split, I made my way over to the receptionist. She was busy talking to a security guard, who was more interested in her than the security of the building and its employees. Although I was standing in front of her, she didn't look at me, instead pointing at the visitors signing-in book. Either this place had a high turnover of visitors or the receptionist didn't give a fuck about the company or its work.

After scrawling my name, I glanced at the security guard: military-style Magnum boots, incredibly well polished without a single scuff mark on them, a Help for Heroes charity band on his wrist. My guess was this guy liked the perceived power status that he thought he got from being a security guard, but the lack of creases or scratches in his boots made me immediately think he didn't do his job. He still hadn't looked at me.

Shit, Tom! What the fuck, stop this right now. You're here for an entry-level IT support job, not to find a target or to give a method for an entry recce of the building. That life is done.

Done.

Waiting patiently for GI Joe to finish his one-way flirting with the receptionist, I desperately tried to hide the frustration building inside me. If you have a job, no matter if you hate it or not, you do it to the best of your ability. It's not hard, is it?

Eventually she looked up. 'Can I help you?'

Obviously you can, fuck's sake.

'Yeah, I'm here for an interview, trainee—'

'Up the stairs, you can join the others.'

This place had a high turnover of staff then. I could be wrong and this could be a rapid expansion move from the company, requiring a lot more staff quickly, but the way the employees didn't take pride in themselves or the company spoke volumes.

Wait a minute, am I the odd one out here? Is this how all workplaces feel? People just come to work for the pay and that's it, no pride? Surely Google's headquarters aren't like this, or Apple's?

Walking up the stairs, I saw thirteen people all sitting on chairs in a narrow corridor, obviously waiting to be interviewed. Most of them looked like nervous teenagers, a few seemed to be in their early twenties. I was by far the oldest. Taking an empty chair, I caught the eye of the young guy I was sitting next to.

'Are you waiting for the interview?'

'Yes. Trainee Tech support.'

Same role. Hopefully there were enough jobs for us all. On my details for this interview the email said to arrive for 0830 hours. I was guessing everyone got the same timing. It was now a waiting game.

In front of me was another keypad-protected door, but this one was solid, no glass. The security pad was different too. Watching three people going into the room beyond, I found myself checking the procedure. The pass card was pressed onto the electronic pad on the wall next to the door. A green LED on the pad prompted a six-figure pin, which looked to be unique to the pass holder, as all three people used a different pin code: 187345, 567125 and 900364. Once the correct pin was entered, another green LED lit up and the door was unlocked, allowing the pass holder to pull it open towards them.

The door was obviously held shut with multiple magnetic locks. In this type of building it would be fairly easy to get through this door without a pass; you would only need to cut the power and back-ups to allow you into the room beyond, as it also acted as a fire door. It was not designed to stop armed robbers from getting in. It was more than likely meant to act as a layer of security to protect the data inside. I was guessing it would be IT support for some sort of infrastructure company; energy, transport, perhaps even the NHS. Something like that.

The interviews weren't lasting long and as the people came out I tried to read their faces. Good interview or bad? Did they get offered a job on the spot? So far, the six people I'd seen leave seemed indifferent. The seventh was a young guy in a bright-yellow tie who puffed out a deep breath the moment he walked through the door. He was very young, seventeen, at a push eighteen years old. His trousers were too big for him too. As he walked past those of us still waiting to go in, his shoulders sinking, two obviously very confident guys looked at each other and smirked at this guy's appearance. In their opinion, he shouldn't be here.

Mr Yellow Tie noticed this reaction to him and his eyes welled up with tears. *Fuck. He can't have been offered the job.* To make things worse for him, he stepped on a loose lace from his left shoe, which instantly snapped, raising more smirks from the cocky twats. Yellow Tie kept walking, something in him refusing to wipe his eyes. He was holding a massive amount of emotion back.

I watched him walk past me, his whole body language that of someone who had given up, but as he started down the stairs, which curved, and his face came into view again, I could see he was still refusing to wipe the tears from his eyes.

Bollocks. Something deep in my gut was forcing me to go

and see if this kid was OK. What if they called my name and I missed the interview? I could blame it on needing the toilet. It wouldn't take long to have a quick word. Cover story first.

Nudging the guy sat next to me I said, 'If they call for Tom, can you tell them I've just nipped to the toilet? Is that OK?'

'Sure, will do.'

Rushing downstairs, I saw Yellow Tie walking through the reception doors into the car park. Trying not to make too much of a scene, I moved as quickly as I could without looking like I was sprinting.

Outside and within touching distance of Yellow Tie, I called out, 'Hey mate, you OK?'

He turned around, a bit startled, but obviously recognized me. Still trying to hide his emotions, he said, 'Yeah, fine. I'm just going to get picked up by my mum.'

He had to be straight out of school. I could see his bottom lip twitch, maybe at the mention of his mother. He was about to break down here, poor fucker. It felt like this was the first time he'd been let loose in the big wide world. Kind of like me, really. This whole standing on your own two feet trying to build a career was completely alien to both of us.

Before I could get my first words out he broke down, just as another employee walked past us through the car park. An older guy, probably senior management, he noticed Yellow Tie but kept moving, not wanting to get involved with a couple of strangers. I needed to get this kid to his mother. Seeing the suffering on his face was really getting to me.

'Come on mate, where is your mum picking you up?'

Unable to talk, he pointed towards the shop I'd gone into earlier.

'OK, come on.' I needed to keep him talking. *Fuck*. I had to get back for my interview but I could spare another couple of minutes, hopefully. 'Do you live around here then?'

'Yeah, just finished college.'

'What course did you do?'

'IT. I really wanted this job. I need . . .' He broke down again before he could finish what he wanted to say.

I could see a woman pulling up in a battered Ford Fiesta.

'Is that your mum there, mate?'

Wiping his tears away, he nodded. I couldn't work out if he was happy to see his mother or not.

'Listen mate, you're better than working here. This place doesn't give a fuck about you or me or anyone else in there. You dodged a bullet, mate. I promise you there is a better job on more money out there for you. Just keep pushing.'

Yellow Tie was starting to take this on board as we got to his mum's car. She was looking slightly concerned, probably noticing my serious face and her son crying. Opening the door for him, I bent down and tried to do my best to explain what was going on.

'Hi, we were both interviewing for the job in there. It's not going great, they don't seem to care about people and it's upset him a bit.' Turning back to Yellow Tie, I added, 'But mate, remember what I said, don't stop chasing it down, you've got so much more to offer than working here. I wish I had your qualifications!'

A smile crept over his face and his mum affectionately ruffled his hair.

Seeing he was in good hands, I ran back into the building and up the stairs. I noticed that the guy I had been sitting next to was no longer there, just as my name was called from behind a half-open door.

The interview room was small, no desk, three chairs. One for me which would put the door behind my back, not ideal. *Fuck, Tom, relax! You're here for a job interview. That part of your life is done. Focus!*

The woman and man interview combo were already sitting down in front of me.

'Hi, nice to meet you,' I said, holding my hand out to them both and doing my best to come across as professional.

'Can you close the door please, Tom, and take a seat,' the woman said.

The interview started with a description of what the position was – IT support for any number of organizations. So when someone in a fairly large company couldn't connect their printer to their laptop or they forgot their password then they rang someone here. I desperately tried to stop focusing on the details. The guy was wearing his watch on his right wrist, which most likely, but not definitely, made him left-handed. The woman kept messing with her pen and alternated from tapping it lightly against her clipboard to biting the end, suggesting she was either desperate for a cigarette or was trying to give up.

I tried to distract myself by interacting and asking

questions about the job, but there was no disguising that the interview wasn't going well. I kept getting hit with questions like 'We have people straight out of college with two years' IT training. Why should we take you over the many others that have these qualifications?' and 'It looks like you took a big step back on your CV to drive trucks.'

I wasn't driving fucking trucks, I was keeping people like you alive! I wanted to shout it out, to rip up my CV and tell them that I'd got something to offer if they would just give me a chance. But I didn't. I swallowed my pride once again and tried to be as humble as possible. Just as I was explaining how motivated I was to learn and contribute there was a knock on the door and the older guy who had passed Yellow Tie and me in the car park walked in.

He stopped in his tracks when I stood up to greet him, holding a firm hand out.

'Hi, I'm Tom. Interviewing for Tech Support.'

'Yes, nice to meet you. I'm Alexander, Director of Operations. I saw you with that boy outside? Was he OK?'

Perfect, this was my wedge. I needed to drive this opening wide now, as fast as I could. 'Yes, he was obviously very upset. I just wanted to make sure he got picked up OK.'

He clearly had a different attitude to the two interviewers and was a lot more personable. *Hold your ground, Tom. You've got him now. Hold.*

'Great. Good spirit.' Releasing my hand, he turned to the two interviewers. 'Can you both pop into my office later?'

Placing a solid pat on my shoulder, Alexander continued, 'And welcome Tom to the team, get him started straight away, yes?'

The woman responded with a surprised but enthusiastic 'of course'. As Alexander left, the two interviewers shared an eye-rolling glance they didn't think I could see before attaching fake smiles to their faces and telling me to be back on Monday for an eight o'clock start.

Thankfully Alexander had come into the interview just in time. I'd be starting on minimum wage, but hopefully if I was quick to learn and worked harder than anyone else I would have opportunities to progress.

When I got home I was pleased to be able to give Lucy the news that we would have some stability and she could rely on me. I never felt any pressure from her to be any different – that came from within, the need to provide and be the dad I never had. It was tough to accept that I was right back at the bottom of the pile, older than most going into that position, but if it meant putting food on the table and keeping a roof over my family's head, I would shovel shit for a living.

The weekend came around quickly. We spent the majority of our time finding cheap smart shirts and a few ties – office clothes I'd never needed before. This was it, the new start, solid family life.

Once I'd met the desk manager, who was waiting for me in reception, I was shown to my desk and sat with a 'trainer', who was supposed to show me the ropes. Exactly what my role would be. Was supposed to be.

I didn't have a problem being taught a new skill by someone

much younger – this guy could do everything on the computer in front of me and knew all the short cuts – but I quickly realized the job title 'technical support' was massively misleading. This was a call centre that had the ability to either reset passwords or tell someone to switch off their computer and turn it on again, and if that didn't solve their issue we could escalate it to actual technical IT support. But none of that mattered. I had a job, a real one. That potentially could lead on to bigger things. And despite my trainer showing more interest in using Tinder than training me, I made the decision to keep my mouth shut and work hard. It was the one thing I could do that would make me stand out to the managers here.

The end of the first week came quickly and I felt I was finding my feet. This company was clearly run to maximize profits, which is only right, but when it's done at the expense of the employees on the desks and the client being charged for our 'support' then it's obviously not right at all.

The company had to work to strict call-answer quotas, so every person sat at a computer would have a stream of calls coming into their headset. I naturally wanted to get through to each call quickly, helping the person on the other line as fast and efficiently as possible – just like in the surveillance teams, when if you're asking for help on the radio then you should get that help instantly.

But unlike MI5, this IT company didn't think about how we took those calls from their clients. Most – but not all – were UK- or US-based. Some companies had thousands of employees all working in different time zones. The busy periods were often when those clients started work, then on their dinner break and again just before they finished work. We'd be taking around 300 calls a day each, sometimes more.

As that first Friday came to a close, I made the decision to ask my line manager if there could be a way of streamlining the process of how we answered calls. I sat down with her as my shift ended, which really annoyed her because she wanted to leave early, but I made sure I was heard by her manager too.

'UK calls come in at nine in the morning. We get hammered and then we are dead until dinner time, between twelve and two, when UK calls come in again just as New York is starting work, then we are quiet until tea time when we have a shift change, UK clients are hammering us with calls just as New York employees are on their dinner ringing in too. There's a quicker way to handle this, I think, which would save the company money and give the clients a better service. Plus it would reduce the stress on the guys in here.'

I went on to explain how we could stagger the shift patterns to make sure we had double the amount of employees taking calls at our busy periods and using the people who looked after the Australian and Italian clients to help out too, when they were completely quiet. It would even out all the workload between us, the clients wouldn't notice anything except a better service and it would reduce the amount of downtime we experienced. I got shut down straight away.

'How long you been here?'

'This is my first week. I'm just trying to help, it wouldn't take much effort and it would be better for everyone.' I said it with the best humble smile I could muster.

It was met with eye rolling and a hand from both my line manager and her boss. 'Your job is to answer the phones. Leave the important stuff to us.'

They walked right past me like my opinion no longer mattered. That was the end of that.

Important stuff? You've no fucking idea what important is, I thought.

When I got home, Lucy could tell how pissed off I was. I just couldn't understand the mentality of people working in the same company either not giving a shit about the work they did, or treating fellow employees like dogs. Listen, obey, but don't step out of line or get ahead of yourself.

We made the decision that night to look for something else, another career path with some progression. Thankfully being in employment makes it easier to find another job. I made contact with a recruitment company that specializes in placing ex-military personnel in suitable roles. Speaking to them on my dinner break the following Monday, I started the process for a fast-track management programme for a fast food restaurant. It was not my thing at all, but I could see the potential and the recruitment guy was actually very honest. 'You'll hate it for a couple of years but at the end of it you're looking at becoming a manager with great prospects afterwards.'

So I took the job and started on the scheme two weeks later. As with any fast-track management programme, you learn the job from the ground up, which meant flipping burgers and dipping a basket of fries into the huge cooking vats. Everyone in the restaurant knew I was ex-military, I just made sure no one ever found out exactly what I did.

I'd get a whole host of the typical questions you'd expect from teenagers talking to an ex-soldier in a work environment: 'Have you ever killed anyone?' 'Did you go to Iraq and Afghanistan?' 'Why did you quit?'

The last question always drove me nuts. Soldiers don't leave the forces by 'quitting'. Quitting is when someone stops going to the gym after three days, having signed up in the new year vowing to get fit for the summer.

I stuck to the standard line that I was in the engineers, and that I didn't see any combat because I was part of a regiment that repaired the older vehicles so the lads could use them overseas. A very busy but rewarding job, knowing that the kit is going to help the guys out. It sounded plausible and entirely boring, which made the questions stop. In reality I had no fucking idea if a unit like that even existed.

I spent months pretending I enjoyed learning how the kitchen worked, what sauces and dressing went on which burgers and how to run the drive-through window, which in fairness to the staff there does take some degree of multitasking. I also realized that the fast-track management scheme was in reality a smokescreen to bring in management without giving them the same pay.

Despite not coming from a catering background at all, I could see there were obvious savings to be made. One example of that was the ice cream machine. Customers could ask for a variety of different toppings. The staff, under the pressure of getting orders fulfilled quickly, would always put at least twice as much topping on the ice cream as they were supposed to and would spill even more, which in the summer in a busy restaurant would be lost profits.

I suggested to the manager that a quick fix would be to have a dispensing machine that would deposit the exact amount of topping, with no mess. The cost would be around £250, but that piece of equipment would be paid for by increased profits in about six hours on a busy day.

I was met with an unwavering, 'We can't afford any new equipment right now.' A restaurant that turns over £4 million a year can't afford £250 to make a hundred times that in its first year? I put a lot of similar suggestions forward to increase profits while reducing the stress on the staff, but in the end it all came down to empire building. People crushing others just to stay one step ahead. I hated this environment but it was one I quickly realized is fairly common in the wider world.

I stayed at the drive-through, flipping burgers, while searching for a new job. I didn't feel superior to anyone there, that's not who I am. I just wanted more. I needed higher targets to achieve. It would have been easy to slip into resentment and anger but I had confidence this job wouldn't be forever. There was an opportunity out there and I would find it.

EPILOGUE

ONCE A SPY . . .

It wasn't my idea to be a writer – I bumped into someone from my old life who was having a meeting with his literary agent.

'Tom, you should write a book,' he said. The agent looked interested.

'Yeah, I could do that,' I replied confidently. I am dyslexic and actually doubted I could write a chapter let alone an entire book but I wasn't going to admit to that. I'd figure it out later.

I believe we make our own luck and this was the opportunity I'd been waiting for. As a way of earning a living it is a big improvement on flipping burgers or working in a call centre. In almost every way it has been incredibly positive. The only negative is that coming forward has meant there has to be an increased level of security around my identity. I would make an attractive target for hostile intelligence agencies. Nothing is more important than keeping my family safe.

On the school run, I always take note of the cars behind me, paying particular attention to the vehicles two or three back. Are they moving naturally with the traffic or anticipating my next change in direction? Taking the turn for my

285

street, I keep an eye on my mirrors, not to watch for any vehicle coming with me, but to watch the heads of the people inside the cars. Is anyone looking down the street as they drive past the end of my road and are they talking? Either could mean they were giving others a change of direction. A classic telltale sign you're being followed.

On this particular afternoon only one car in the line of traffic stood out, a red Ford Fiesta driven by a woman with shoulder-length brown hair who was looking down my street as she drove past. Her car had been three behind me for a mile or so, since the last roundabout. Her lips were moving as she drove past. Not concrete evidence I was being watched, but enough to heighten my awareness.

Pulling up outside the house, I knew it was important to keep my body language the same as it always would be. Smoke and mirrors. I got out of the car and walked around to my son's side to unclip him out of his booster seat. Using the natural look through the window, I could keep an eye on the top of the street for anyone on foot or for vehicles that were standing out. The red Fiesta had put me on alert. I just wasn't sure if it was valid or if my PTSD was making a comeback.

I paused slightly to talk to my son as I pretended to be distracted while getting the house key into the lock. I used the split second to listen to my environment before walking through the safety of the door. Any changes in engine noises, slowing down or speeding up, engines being switched off or doors opening, footsteps. Anything that I could latch onto.

I needed to make sure my family was safe. If we were being

watched I had to get them out of here and quickly. But first I had to identify if there was a threat and how big it was.

'Can you watch little legs for a minute?'

While Lucy took his rucksack, I made my way to the back door, pausing briefly to take my grab bag, which was tucked away underneath the kitchen sink. It contained everything I needed to help me identify if we were under surveillance, and crucially, the items we needed to disappear. I knew my bag was complete, having checked it religiously just two days earlier.

'Tom, everything OK?' Lucy knew the hidden bags were only to be used in certain situations.

'I'm just going to check something, I'll be back in a few minutes. I'm sure it's fine though. Can you lock the doors and switch the lights on? If I'm not back in ten minutes, go straight to Big Blue.'

Lucy has been through my therapy with me. She knows the triggers and signs of hyper-vigilance but also knows what I used to do. From her perspective, it must be a difficult balance to find – should she try to stop me if the danger could be real?

Taking one of the emergency tops next to my small bag, I changed the colour of my profile. Then I moved towards the bottom of the garden and vaulted the fence to cut through onto the road behind our street. I needed to identify anyone who was watching the front of our house or our car. Squeezing through the gap between two houses, I made it onto the road and joined several people at the bus stop. Thankfully, this was a busy route. Staying close to the group, I boarded the next bus, which went further down the street and close to the bottom edge of the road my house is on.

It was only a short journey, less than a minute, but absolutely vital as it gave me a protected view of what might be going on in my area. At first I couldn't see anything out of the ordinary. The people on the bus were minding their own business, pedestrians on the street were moving normally. I even recognized the drunk locals returning from the shop with that afternoon's super-strength lager.

Getting ready to leave the bus at the next stop, I stood just behind the driver's shoulder. That's when I saw the car parked at the end of my road, two men inside. When a group of people came to the front ready to get off, I tucked myself in the middle of them, hood up to make it look like I was protecting myself from the rain that had just started to come down.

Making the turn towards my street, I knew I was about three minutes' walk away from my front door. In those three minutes I had to decide whether or not this was a situation I needed to get my family out of.

Keep moving, get home.

The driver of the stationary car was switched on and saw me approaching, cracking his window down to speak to me.

'All right mate, you live around here?'

Nodding back, I put my arm over the top of the door onto the roof, keeping my right knee further back from my left just in case things went wrong quickly and he tried to get out.

'Seen any mopeds around?' the driver asked. Now I was close I could recognize the outline of a Kevlar vest underneath a waterproof jacket. He wasn't interested in me, and I could see from the equipment within the car that they were plain-clothes police officers. The passenger was on the phone back to command by the sounds of it.

'I haven't, is that what you're here for?'

'Yeah, we've seen a few come towards this area so we are talking to the locals and seeing if they can help us. But we're trying to keep a low profile so we don't scare them off.'

Now I knew my family was safe, I needed to get back to them before Lucy left for our pre-arranged emergency location.

'Sorry, I haven't seen any today.'

'Fair enough.'

As I walked away, I could hear the unmarked police car leaving. Two minutes to get home before Lucy would be out of the door, protecting our family.

Arriving at the front door, the house looked busy – lights on, no sign of Lucy about to bolt to safety. I gave a knock she'd recognize before I unlocked the door. In the hall, I saw her with our son and our larger grab bags. Instantly, she relaxed.

'What was it?'

'Local police, just needed to make sure.'

Trying to instantly get back to normality, I was not aware of the damage I was doing until Lucy grabbed my arm to stop me walking away. 'Are you OK?'

The concern on her face stopped me in my tracks. Was I spiralling or did I react rationally to the picture in front of me, before ruling out a potential threat? I knew I was struggling to adjust to civilian life. Normality was something I had craved for years, but now it was here I didn't know what to do with it. Good mental health takes the same care as physical health – you have to take daily preventative measures to make sure you stay fit. But it's hard not to lapse into a hyper-viligant state when I've spent a decade hunting down some of the most dangerous people in the country. I can't unlearn what I know.

Whenever I enter a building for a meeting, I still naturally pay attention to the numbers people are putting into keypads, the processes on reception, if there's a back door. When I meet people from a similar background in a restaurant or bar there's always a fight to grab the seats that allow the best view of the room, to the point we're nearly sitting on each other's laps sometimes. If I'm walking around in London, I choose the side of the road facing oncoming traffic so I can see if there's a moped looking to nick a phone or an extremist in a car looking to kill pedestrians. A few seconds' warning can make all the difference. I try not to let it take over my life to the point where it's getting daft, but these small measures give me a sense of a control. So does staying positive and focused on my goals. I don't spend time on regrets – I survived some rough times as a kid but you can't let your past dictate your future. I had a job I loved and when that came to an end I kept looking until I found a new purpose.

And yet . . . even though my life is really busy I still miss

everyone in Green Team and the wider teams. To be surrounded by people who can rely on you and who you can rely
on in return, without question, without hidden agenda, all
pulling together in the same direction, is a rare thing. I have
never found that anywhere else and probably never will. I also
miss the admin staff who would look after our expenses,
hotels and cover ID. I even miss the jobsworth in our stores
who would prefer to keep stuff in stock rather than hand it
out, 'just in case someone needs it!'

But I never doubt that everyone is doing their best to protect us, and they are the best in the fucking world!

ACKNOWLEDGEMENTS

I want to thank:

My wife for always being my one true constant. Without you I'd have been lost a long time ago.

Luigi and Ingrid for having incredible patience and faith during the clearance process and supporting me throughout.

Everyone in the Security Service, especially the ones in my team for giving me help when I needed it.

And Paul, my brother, for recognizing my value and giving me an opportunity no one else would.

AVAILABLE NOW

CAPTURE
OR
KILL

Turn the page to read an extract from
Tom Marcus' action-packed thriller featuring
tortured MI5 operative Matt Logan.

PROLOGUE

Standing in the doorway of my flat, I take one last look. It's clean and orderly, the home of a righteous man. And yet, beneath the surface, I know it could be defiled. There may be bugs hidden somewhere, spies listening to my every word. Well, if so, they will have heard many prayers, but not our plans. I put my phone on the shelf by the door before walking out onto the landing. With your phone, they can track you wherever you go. And of course, they can record what you say. Which is why Mohammed and I never communicate electronically. If we need to meet, we fix the place the night before, during last prayers at the mosque. Only the two of us know the plan. We never meet in the same place twice and never inside a building or an open space like a park. Following these rules keeps us alive, and lets us hope we may, in the future, live in a different world from this corrupted one.

I walk down the stairwell and leave my block of flats, walking calmly but purposefully, watching for anyone who looks out of place or who is paying too much attention to me. I see no spies, but I have to be sure. Before crossing the street, I wait at the traffic lights, looking both ways. The light changes to green, but I don't cross yet, instead I wait for cars or people to react to me, stopping suddenly or changing direction. Still no sign of anyone.

Moving onto the other side of the road lets me look up and down the street, checking for anyone hiding in their cars. There's a phone shop on the corner and I check that the owner is alone before entering. He nods to me as I walk past the counter and out of the side door into a narrow alley, which leads to the back of the houses behind. If anyone follows me down here, I will know they are spies.

The alley is dark. I put my hood up and look back onto the street. In the darkness I am like a ghost; no one can see me. But the end of the alley is lit up like a TV. Anyone looking down here to try and see me would stand out.

Still clean. I turn and walk to the other end of the alley, away from the lights of the main road, until I reach the bottom of a grimy stairwell. I can see the silhouette of Mo's bulky frame, ambling towards the same pre-arranged spot from the opposite direction, I greet him.

'As-salāmu 'alaykum.'

'Wa'alaykumu s-salām.' Mo replies as we keep our voices to a whisper. No one could be listening to us here. But there's a reason neither of us has ever been arrested or even spoken to by the police. We are always careful, always following the rules we have made for ourselves.

'Mo, the two brothers I told you about yesterday, I believe they are ready. It is time.'

'And we trust them? We must assume they are being followed.'

'I gave instructions to them at first prayers this morning how to disappear. They've been trained well.'

'And you're sure they are capable of executing the plan?'

'I'm controlling what they do at each stage. Only we know the full plan. But they will do their part. Then we can move to the caliphate.'

'Then proceed, brother.'

I embrace Mohammed quickly before we go our separate ways. Our meeting has lasted less than a minute. Now I need to get to work, to fulfil my part in society, hiding in plain sight. It's only a two-minute walk from here, but I don't take the fastest route. Instead I start off in the opposite direction, turning back on myself to make sure I am still not being followed. Finally, I see my place of work, shining brightly, a picture of Western opulence.

Walking through the entrance, I'm met with the familiar face of the receptionist. The way she flaunts herself is degrading, the usual garish red lipstick as familiar as her greeting.

'Doctor Khan, how are you?'

I don't show my disgust. 'I'm very well, thank you.'

'I hope you're ready for the night shift. We're short-staffed again.'

'I'm always ready,' I reply, waving a hand as I walk past her.

I smile to myself. She has no idea how ready I am.

1

Stumbling, a junkie badly in need of a fix. It's raining and my filthy jeans and ripped parka are already soaked through. Rainwater squeezes in through the holes in my trainers, and I start coughing – a nasty rattling that makes me sound as if I'm properly sick. Through half-closed eyes I can see the abandoned building, but I don't head straight for it. Instead I lurch into a corner of the disused park opposite and collapse under a tree that gives at least some protection from the downpour. Surrounded by bits of old tinfoil that glint in the passing lights of the odd car, I catch sight of a broken syringe and an old burned spoon. Under the penetrating smell of cat shit, I can detect the faint but distinct odour of heroin, like rancid vinegar burning its way into my nose. Flipping the hood of my parka up with a grimy hand, I fix my gaze on the door of the building opposite.

'From Zero Three, I have direct on the house, I can give them away, but can't go with.'

Talking into my radio, my voice is hushed but clear.

Now my team knows I'm in position. The targets are inside,

and as soon as they move, we can keep control of them. All I have to do now is what junkies do best: wait. My cover is good – no one would believe the foul-smelling, dishevelled wreck slouched under the tree, surrounded by syringes and other junkie paraphernalia, could be an undercover surveillance officer. Which is fortunate, as in this run-down area of Birmingham, the drug gangs pretty much own the streets, and if they made you as police, you'd be dead. And the truth is, most surveillance officers wouldn't be capable of doing it in a convincing way. It's one thing looking and smelling the part: anyone can put on piss-soaked jeans and a grimy T-shirt, leave off shaving or washing for a few days, get some nicotine stains on their fingers and dirt under their nails. It's another thing to walk and talk like a down and out, to think like someone who survives on the streets. To really *live* the part.

For me, though, it comes naturally. I grew up on streets like this. I learned the hard way how to survive. And though, thank God, I never became an addict, I spent a lot of time with people who did. Which made me a unique asset within the intelligence services. I wasn't comfortable working in posh areas like Chelsea, trying to blend in with the upper classes, but out here, getting into the mindset of a hardcore junkie, was no problem at all. Which might have explained my nickname during training: 'Tramp'.

They didn't call me that for long, though.

'Roger that Zero Three, you have Zero Eight in close to support you and Charlie Seven Seven has taken note of all the vehicle registration numbers in the area, base acknowledge.'

The team leader, Lee, already had control of this operation, making sure the operations officers back at Thames House were in the loop but also responding instantly to us.

'Base roger, we've checked those VRNs, no results showing on the grid, For information Iron Sword last seen dark jacket, light blue jeans and Stone Fist green jacket, black bottoms. And for information we don't have any technical assistance on this, no tracking at all.'

Those were the code names for the brothers, and having no other way of tracking these two other than our team following them, it meant if we didn't keep hold of them, they'd disappear. As a surveillance officer, that was your worst nightmare. Especially since we suspected that was exactly what they were planning to do. But right now, I knew the rest of the team would be finding all sorts of places to conceal themselves, waiting for me to send the stand-by signal over the radio. The brothers would have to show capabilities we hadn't seen before to escape our iron grip. It was only the bosses, the people who gave us our orders, I sometimes worried about. The police are already becoming accountable for their actions in open courts. I just hope we have enough protection higher up so the same thing doesn't start happening to us.

Keeping my eyes on the front door, I shuffle over as a group of half a dozen locals appears, parking themselves under my tree. This is when I need to keep playing my part for all its worth; if one of them gets the idea I'm not who I'm pretending to be, it's game over. But they seem too drunk or wasted to take much notice, and fortunately they have plenty of pills, and a plastic bottle of cheap cider they're passing around, so hopefully they're not going to bother me. My attention is still focused on the door, and these lowlifes are not my concern. They could start murdering each other and I wouldn't budge. But we're trained to notice everything when we're on a job, to take in every detail, in case something is out of place, something isn't right, and we need to change our plans immediately to avoid being compromised. So while most people would just try to shut them out and pretend they weren't there, I find myself noting every detail about them.

From the state of their hair and fingernails, they're clearly living on the streets and have been for some time, stuck in the vicious cycle of searching for their next fix and then finding somewhere relatively safe to come back round. The woman in this group of six addicts, in her early twenties I'd guess, though you could be forgiven for thinking she was twice that from her gaunt and haggard features, is so off her face her ripped tracksuit bottoms have slipped halfway down her arse, showing off a ragged thong which clearly hasn't been washed in a while. She stumbles over and collapses in a heap next to me as one of the men starts urinating behind our tree.

A small voice inside my head asks me what the fuck I'm doing sitting under a tree in the rain, getting splashback from a homeless drug addict, but suddenly I can see a blade of light creeping from behind the door of the house as it slowly opens, and I focus my mind on what I'm here for. Wasted as they are, my new friends are too close for me to risk talking on my radio, so I'll have to use the covert messaging method instead.

The door opens fully, and I can see the side profile of a male coming out. He's talking to someone still inside the house and is being handed something that looks at this distance like the pistol grip of a small weapon, I can't be sure, and I can't yet see if they're our targets. I catch myself frowning in concentration as I try to make out who they are, and tell myself to relax my body position, to not give away that I'm interested in the house. Then a second figure leaves the house and turns to face in my direction.

It's one of the brothers. I have to alert the team but can't talk. Using the covert message system, I give the stand-by signal.

'STANDBY STANDBY heard! Zero Three, are both Iron Sword and Stone Fist out?'

My team leader knows the right questions to ask me, but I need to alert the team to this small unknown item that looked dark and small enough to be a pistol.

Responding, I use our covert message to tell the team leader yes.

'Roger that Zero Three, both out. Are they walking away from you south?'

I message back a negative, as I can see the brothers and they're walking fast, directly towards me on the other side of the road. Even with the rain and the crappy street lighting I can tell it's them because of the distinctive scars on their faces, mementos of their last prison stay. Something's definitely different about them, though, since the last time we deployed on them. They've suddenly become super-vigilant, looking at everything, complete three-sixty awareness. I tell myself not to react, not to tense up. Just live your cover.

There's some tension showing back at base, though.

'Stations from Base, we have nothing on this at all, no eavesdropping or electronic.'

'Base roger from Team Leader, we're on it. Zero Three, are they walking north?'

Still unable to talk, I reply with a yes, 'Roger that, Iron Sword and Stone Fist are walking north, north on Lozells Street towards Wills Street. Zero Eight acknowledge?'

'Zero Eight roger and in position.'

Shit. I've got to find a way of transmitting openly here. My team needs to know how aware both targets are, and if they are armed we could do with some police backup. But I sure as hell can't do it now; the brothers are getting closer to my position, walking faster in the rain. As they hurry past, one of the addicts hauls himself to his feet and shouts out. The brothers both turn instantly, and the addict gestures to the woman, now halfway decent again and slumped against the tree. He mumbles something, most of it complete garbage. It's got the word 'fuck' in it. He's trying to sell her for sex. The brothers have other things on their mind and start moving on, but not before their eyes briefly lock onto me. I know I'm good, there's nothing about my appearance or behaviour that can give away the fact that I'm not who I'm pretending to be, but all the same I feel a small surge of adrenaline. This is where it could all go wrong. This is where I could let down the team and fuck the entire operation.

One of the brothers pulls the other by the arm and they're gone. Now I just have to wait until both targets are under someone else's control and I can get out of here. But right now, I can only get the team leader to interrogate me using the covert messaging system, in the world's deadliest game of yes or no.

Sending a message out onto the net, I'm hoping the team leader is on the ball and starts asking the right questions, quickly.

'Zero Three is that you?'

Perfect, now I've got to get this going and quickly.

'Roger, have the targets stopped prior to the junction?'

Fuck. This was going to take too long, time we didn't have. I needed to get the message across right now.

'Yeah. From Zero Eight, I have control of Iron Sword and Stone Fist, both extremely vigilant, Team Leader, this is what Zero Three might have been trying to say. I'd like to give these guys some room.'

Thank God Dexter had taken control of the two brothers, and had already spotted that they were acting differently. Now I could get away from here and change my profile, get out of these piss-stained clothes. My van was parked a few streets away, so it wasn't going to take me long. Hearing the team was in control of the targets and aware of their new behaviour was a huge relief. If we gave them some room, maybe everything was going to be all right.

As long as we didn't give them *too* much room.

'Base, permission?'

The operations officers at Thames House know they have to ask permission from the person in control of the targets, in this case, Dexter, to get onto the net to ask questions or give updates.

'Go ahead, both walking west on Wills Street towards the food market, still very aware and now walking very slowly.'

Their initial brisk walking pace could have been to get them away from Lozells Street, a risky place to be at night even for them, but I couldn't help thinking this was classic operational behaviour, speeding up, then rounding a corner and slowing down, trying to catch out any surveillance.

'Thanks, crews for information, we'd like you to keep a tight control of the brothers, intelligence from G Branch is suggesting they are going to try and drop off the grid. Base out.'

'Roger that, crews close in and we'll rotate it around as much as we can. Back to you Zero Eight.'

Slowly getting to my feet, using the trunk of the tree to slide up, I listen to Dexter as he gives a running commentary on what the brothers are doing, their appearance, their alertness levels. I step over the wannabe pimp, who's got a stillness about him I know well. His rigid breathing corpse, complete with a small bag of bright-yellow pills poking out of the top of his socks, is waiting to metabolize the chemicals that have incapacitated all of the group. The woman is out of it, curled up in a pool of her own piss under the tree. Now that the brothers are gone, I can afford to see them as fellow human beings rather than bit-part players in a drama of my own creation. I hated seeing people like that. I know from experience it was probably one wrong decision years ago that led them to being here in this state, that what they needed was a helping hand to haul them out of the shit. But although I could sympathize more than most, I was no social worker. My job was to stop terrorists killing civilians. If the civilians chose to kill themselves by putting a needle in their arm, there was nothing I could do about it.

Ducking under the low branches and out into the rain, now easing to fine drizzle, I shuffle across the street and along the path, heading south past the house the brothers had left a few minutes ago. My van was only around the next two corners, but I had to keep living my cover. Head down, shoulders dropped, I manage a quick glance at the house. In complete darkness, it looks like any other derelict building in the neighbourhood. Until you clock the steel sheeting over the boarded-up windows. And while the door is covered in graffiti just like the others on the street, underneath it is solid steel too.

I slow down, pretending to have a good cough. But the truth is, I'm using the moment to gain as much useful information as I can. What's missing? What should be here but isn't? What's here but shouldn't be? I only have a few seconds before I'll start to look suspicious. Think! Nothing ground level. Nothing—Bingo! That's it. A very small CCTV camera high up near the roof line, tucked away under the guttering on the church on the opposite side of the road.

The fact it's clearly an off-the-shelf type of camera you can buy anywhere, powered by a battery, instantly tells me it's not an official part of the CCTV network installed by the council. It's pointing directly at one house in this row, which means it was highly likely put there by whoever is operating out of this house. A small wireless aerial at the top suggests it's probably transmitting wirelessly.

A massive amount of effort has gone into making it look like a regular derelict building, but with added features designed to keep squatters out, meaning there were only two plausible explanations: either this was a drug-money house, or some sort of weapons stash. Given the brothers' history of drug dealing, it could be either, but I'm betting on the latter. All the more reason not to let these guys fall off the grid. Rounding the corner, resisting the urge to speed my shuffle into a fast walk, I'm keen to get back to the van and send a message to Base about the CCTV. Most people in my situation would think I'd gotten lucky here, but the truth is our teams always live our cover no matter what the circumstances. You'll always be caught on camera, but if you are living your cover properly then it doesn't matter. Anyone watching this camera feed would see another druggy. Not an MI5 operator.

'All stations Zero Eight, hold back hold back, that's both IN IN to a takeaway chicken shop on the corner of Church Street, any vehicle call sign get this?'

Dexter's right, asking for vehicle support. When any target goes into a building it becomes easier for them to sit and watch people outside, and identify people like us.

'Charlie Four Seven has the front door.'

'Stations from Team Leader, I don't want anyone to go inside. Let them breathe for a while.'

We know this chicken shop well. It's a nightmare to cover properly, not in the worst part of the neighbourhood but right on a busy junction with floor-to-ceiling glass windows. In his car, Charlie Four Seven – Imran – has sight of the front door and a clear view inside because of the lighting, but I know he'll be struggling for cover. No one in their right mind sits in a stationary car for long around here.

I have some time to change my profile and get with the follow. I unzip my jacket as I approach the last corner, glancing behind me as I cross the road, as if I'm checking for traffic. I'm still clean, no one following, but anyone watching my van would question a homeless guy getting into it. So, turning the corner, I slip my parka off quickly, straighten the way I walk, take my keys out and walk confidently towards the driver's side, get straight in and pull away. The brothers might not be watching, but surveillance teams always try and leave as little sign as possible when entering and leaving an area. You never know, we could be working here for the next few years. The last thing you want to do is ruin that by wheel-spinning away or sitting there with the engine running right outside someone's house. No one knows better than us: you *never* know who's watching.

'Direct, Charlie Nine permission quick message?'

By switching from my foot call sign to my vehicle call sign, the team will know I'm not pretending to be a drug addict anymore and am in the safety of my van.

'Charlie Four Seven, go ahead no change, still inside facing the counter. Looks like they're ordering.'

'Roger, thanks, Base, the house the brothers left, number 158 Lozells Street, has the appearance of a derelict building with security sheeting on the windows and the door, but there is a CCTV camera tucked under the roofline of the church directly opposite. It's pointing at the front door of the target address. On leaving it looked like Iron Sword was handed a small dark object, couldn't confirm but it looked similar to a pistol grip. Charlie Nine out.'

'Base, roger, all stations acknowledge that the targets could potentially be armed. Thank you.'

As the team all respond to the Ops officer's call from Thames House, confirming they understand the targets could have a weapon on them, the team leader will have got straight on the phone to Base to ask for armed police support.

'From Charlie Four Seven, that's both Iron Sword and Stone Fist now sitting down inside the takeaway with food. Iron Sword has a view straight out of the window for information.'

Driving round in a big circle, I move into a position where I can potentially help my team without being too close in. There's no point in saturating the area, especially when one of the brothers can see directly onto the street, and I know the rest of the team will be holding key routes out of the area too. So far, so good.

'Stations, while we have a lull, security checks please, down the list.'

I know why the team leader is checking on the other operators in the team. In this area, the brothers aren't the only threats we have to worry about. The only people in their cars at this time of night will be dealers or police, and because we've taken great pains not to look like police, we are obvious targets for gangs defending their patch. I can tell by the team's responses as they confirm their positions that the control around the brothers is as tight as can be, and no one is in any bother from the locals.

I keep running my memory back to when the brothers came out of the door. Could the object have just been a big phone, or something else more innocuous than a pistol? It was too hard to tell at that distance, in the rain, at night, but it had still been worth putting it out to the team.

'Charlie Nine, holding the park to the west on Villa Street.'

'Thanks stations, Direct, back to you.'

There is barely a second between transmissions; Imran is clearly desperate to get a message out on the radio.

'STANDBY STANDBY, SPLIT SPLIT! From Charlie Four Seven, that's Iron Sword OUT OUT and walking west-bound towards St George's Park and Villa Street, Stone Fist is northbound, north on Church Street. Team Leader, just before they split, Stone Fist pointed in my direction, looking aggressive. I'm going to have to front this out and hope it wasn't me he was pointing at. If I move away now I'll be bang to rights for sure.'

'Charlie Nine, roger.'

The lull is well and truly over. The brothers are definitely not behaving normally. It could just be drugs paranoia, or it could be they are getting close to their endgame. The trouble is, neither us on the ground nor the intelligence officers back at Thames House have the faintest idea what that endgame is. They had both been serving long prison sentences for firearms offences when they got involved in a fight, which seemed like a deliberate ploy to get them moved to the wing where all the extremists were. Once we knew they had been converted, the agent handlers from G Branch showed massive interest, but in the six months since they'd got out we hadn't been able to figure out what they were doing. All we could be sure of was that they could have done a hell of a lot of planning and preparation in that time.

'From Charlie Nine, I have control of Iron Sword walking westbound on Wills Street, now at the junction of Villa Street. Stations be aware he's just stood at the junction looking slowly at everything in front of him.'

Sat in the van, I can see Iron Sword now. He's calmed down, isn't looking as paranoid, but even at this distance I can see him studying everything; vehicles, houses, the odd pedestrian. The rain isn't bothering him either. He looks as if he knows what he's doing. This is new. The suspicion has gone, replaced by calm certainty, almost as if the brothers have been told they're being watched and it's just a case of finding us. If that's true, things have progressed much further than we thought. And, more to the point, we'll need to be at the top of our game to avoid being compromised.

'Aargh, shit, Charlie Four Seven! Stone Fist has just thrown a brick through my back window. Driving out of the area now.'